SOCIAL EFFICIENCY

SOCIAL EFFICIENCY

A Concise Introduction to
Welfare Economics

PETER BOHM
Department of Economics,
University of Stockholm

A HALSTED PRESS BOOK

JOHN WILEY & SONS
New York – Toronto

First published in the United Kingdom 1973 by
The Macmillan Press Ltd

Published in the U.S.A. and Canada by
Halsted Press
a Division of John Wiley & Sons, Inc.,
New York

Printed in Great Britain

Library of Congress Cataloging in Publication Data

Bohm, Peter, 1935–
    Social efficiency.

    "A Halsted Press book."
    Bibliography: p.
    1. Welfare economics. I. Title.
HB99.3.B58   330.15'5   73-9379
ISBN 0-470-08635-1

To KERSTIN

CONTENTS

PREFACE

In this book, the main elements of *welfare economics* are presented in concise form. Welfare economics is that part of economics that attempts to explain how to identify and arrive at *socially efficient* solutions to the resource allocation problems of the national (or local) economy. Expressed another way, welfare economics tries to reduce the set of alternatives containing the 'best' solution for the economy by eliminating such solutions as can be shown to be inferior to other feasible solutions. The next step—choosing the 'best' or 'optimum' among the alternatives in this reduced set—is a question of subjective values and hence, not within the province of scientific analysis.

The book is primarily intended as a university text for the 'advanced beginner'. I believe that large parts of it, however, are accessible to other readers who have a serious interest in the efficiency problems of the economy. It should be observed that chapters 2, 3 and 4 can each be read independently of the preceding parts of the book. It is difficult, however, to obtain a firm grasp of the contents of the book—and of chapter 1 in particular—without prior elementary knowledge of microeconomic theory: the theory of the economic behaviour of firms and households. (See the list of literature at the end of the book for suggested preliminary reading.)

As indicated, the mode of presentation is brief and concise. Readers who prefer extensive explanations with many examples should therefore turn to other texts. In fact, the book is intended as an alternative to the extensive texts already available, an alternative meant to facilitate a cohesive overview of social efficiency problems in general and to expose the basic similarities among the many problems of resource allocation in the local or national economy.

In the preparation of the book I have benefited from helpful comments by many colleagues. I am indebted to all of them and in particular to William Baumol, William Branson, Alf Carling, Margareta Johannesson, E. J. Mishan and Lewis Taylor. Julie Sundquist has given valuable assistance in the preparation of the English version of the book.

Stockholm   PETER BOHM

INTRODUCTION

The purpose of this book is to give the reader an insight into the meaning of social efficiency, efficient use of a nation's resources, optimal
allocation of resources and similar expressions.

Social efficiency will hardly appear as a straightforward concept to
the non-economist. In certain cases, however, social efficiency coincides
with the more well-known concept of efficiency in a private enterprise,
that is minimum production costs for a certain output, maximum
profits and the like. And in these cases it may truly be said that 'what is
good for General Motors is good for the country'. But in other cases the
two concepts—social and private efficiency—do not coincide at all. This
is liable to cause misunderstandings and even those who are expected to
observe efficiency on a national level (such as politicians and government
agencies) cannot avoid confusing the two concepts. In many countries
this is particularly conspicuous in the field of public transport; bus and
railway communications are shut down owing to losses at the 'firm'
level even in instances where such measures can be shown to be a waste
of resources from the point of view of society as a whole. The reason
for this behaviour is often a belief that businesslike operations are
always in the interest of the country or, at least, in the interest of the
government. And this may be taken as an expression of the fact that
the two efficiency aspects are generally believed to coincide more often
than they actually do.

Social efficiency has also been misunderstood in another way and for
a completely different reason. It is often alleged that efficiency in general
is irrelevant for, or even incompatible with, values such as 'equity',
'high cultural standards', 'healthy environment', etc. As we shall see, it
is more often the other way round; acts aimed at achieving *social*
efficiency can in fact be said to promote more of such values. Briefly
speaking, this is so because social efficiency involves an attempt to take
into account *all* individuals' evaluations of *all* consequences of economic
acts—in other words, not only the direct or purely material consequences
of such acts.

To many people economics seems difficult, even obscure. The main
reason for this impression often turns out to be that the *money* or

financial aspects of the matter tend to be confusing. The crucial economic aspects, however, are generally much easier to grasp if the 'veil of money' is lifted and the problem is looked at in real terms. An example may clarify this proposition: say that a person has bought some pieces of wood for £1 each to build something and it later turns out that he did not need them all. Although it is certainly correct to say that the boards *did* cost £1 each (and that an additional piece would cost that much) this does not normally say anything about the *value* of the remaining boards. The value is determined solely on the basis of the possible ways of using these boards that this person might now think of. Having considered all the alternatives—including that of reselling the boards—he may find that the best one, after all, is to burn them. In that event, if his child comes by looking for something to play with, giving the boards to the child would certainly not entail a real cost of £1 each (the purchase price), but only what they are considered to be worth as fuel. A considerable part of economics and especially the analysis of efficiency problems, is based on a so-called opportunity cost argument of this uncomplicated kind, that is on the value of the best alternative use of a given resource, be it an available commodity, a piece of machinery or an hour of work.

It is an unfortunate fact that the desire to spell out the details of a complex economic reality often makes it difficult to see the scope of the simple principle just mentioned. In an attempt to clarify this principle and to facilitate an overall view of the general problem of social efficiency, the presentation below is made relatively brief and free from examples and elaborate details. This approach is based on a belief that once a bird's eye perspective has been acquired, it will be easier—at least for the patient student—to scrutinise examples and understand real-world situations.

In line with this objective we start by giving a brief account of the main contents of this book.

(1) It can be shown that a certain simple model of an economy— with, among other things, many buyers and sellers of every commodity— can generate situations that are socially efficient in the sense that further changes which benefit all individuals are impossible. This property is not made irrelevant or unimportant by the mere fact that reality always deviates from the assumptions behind the model. As a point of departure it may be superior to the available alternatives, and as an approximation of parts of real-world economic problems it has the virtue of being

simple. Moreover, the conclusions drawn from this model are certainly not unimportant from an historical and political point of view; they form the cornerstone of all propositions concerning the advantages of a market economy and of competition in the economic sphere.

(2) Looking at the assumptions behind the model—the 'perfect market economy' model—we find that the lack of realism is due to the absence of phenomena such as monopoly and other forms of imperfect competition, increasing returns in production, the inability to organise markets for all commodities of interest to consumers, etc. It can be shown that a government interested in efficiency of the type mentioned in point 1 above can neutralise or eliminate such 'imperfections' and achieve efficient states for the economy by means of certain acts of economic policy ('allocation policy').

(3) At the same time, the government may be interested in achieving one particular efficient state and thereby one particular 'income or welfare distribution' among the individuals participating in the economy. Moreover, the government may be dissatisfied with the way the economy behaves even if it *tends* towards the desired state. There are recurring 'accidents' in the form of short-term general unemployment and more enduring employment problems in certain regions or sectors. Economic policy measures are therefore taken also for the purpose of adjusting income distribution and combatting tendencies towards general or local recession. A conflict with the efficiency objective may arise in this pursuit. Moreover, alternative modes of such economic policy may differ in their ability to achieve distribution and stabilisation goals in an efficient way. Thus, there are reasons for observing efficiency aspects of economic policy in general.

(4) Regardless of the actual choice of objectives for economic policy we can feel free to assume that the desired overall state of the economy will be one of maximum efficiency *provided* that certain stabilisation and distribution goals have been met. And *maximum* efficiency should be in the interest of the government (or the individual politician) regardless of the weight it (or he) attaches to these stabilisation and distribution goals. Given this uniform principle a general method can be established for decision-making or policy-making in individual cases of tax changes, new legislation, public investment projects, etc.—a so-called cost–benefit analysis.

These are the four points that will be dealt with in the four chapters of the book. We shall thus show (1) how and in what sense social efficiency can be attained in a 'perfect market economy', (2) how real-world imperfections can be corrected by 'allocation policy', (3) what the relations are between efficiency and economic policy for stabilisation and distribution purposes and (4) what the cost–benefit criterion for public investments and other specific government measures is.

1. SOCIAL EFFICIENCY AND THE PERFECT MARKET ECONOMY

Economics is essentially about economising with scarce resources. The fact that resources are scarce implies that it is necessary to choose among alternative uses—alternative allocations of resources to sectors of production and alternative allocations (or distributions) of output to members of society. Our criterion for 'good' and 'bad' allocations of this kind is based on the following preconditions:

(a) 'Consumption is the goal of all production'. We assume that individuals are not interested in production *per se,* but only in the output of production in terms of immediate or future consumption.

(b) Consumption is evaluated in the light of the explicit preferences and appraisals of the individual members of society ('consumer's sovereignty'). We assume that these preferences are formed on the basis of 'sufficient' information about consumption alternatives. In fact, to begin with, we assume that information is complete ('perfect information'). (Later on, it will be observed that information may be incomplete and that the government may express and enforce a guardian attitude with respect to the consumption pattern exhibited by individual consumers.)

(c) We shall be on the lookout for feasible changes in the economy which would make all consumers better off, or at least make one consumer better off without making others worse off. Obviously, when the possibilities of making such changes are exhausted, we are left with an allocation of resources and output that cannot be altered without someone being made worse off. Such allocations—there may be many—are called Pareto-optimal allocations or socially efficient allocations.

The purpose of this chapter is to indicate the conditions under which allocations of resources and output are Pareto optimal. In order to simplify the presentation we start with a single-period analysis of a barter economy with only two commodities (in section 1.1) and continue by gradually introducing more realistic situations: production with one factor of production (section 1.2), many factors of production and many commodities (section 1.3) and production–consumption in a two-period economy (section 1.5). We then describe the circumstances under which the conditions for Pareto-optimal allocation can be fulfilled in a *market* economy (sections 1.4 and 1.5).

The present chapter provides most of the analytical foundations for the discussion in the subsequent chapters. In order to avoid misunderstandings at this crucial point, the presentation has been made relatively technical and formal. Thus, in the beginning, the reader should be prepared to read rather slowly. It may be added, however, that an understanding of the main parts of later chapters does not require a complete command of the formal analysis of the present chapter. Moreover, it should be pointed out that the main elements of this formal analysis can be obtained in three, to a large extent separate, ways: the diagrammatic approach in the figures of this chapter, the verbal formulation in the text and the explicit mathematical approach in appendix 1, part 1.

1.1   Pareto Optimality in a Pure Barter Economy

An easy starting-point, which nevertheless lends itself to conclusions relevant in more realistic situations, is to assume an economy in which there is no production, only barter between two persons, A and B, who own given quantities of two commodities, 1 and 2. A's initial quantity of commodity 1 is denoted $\bar{x}_{A1}$. The remaining symbols are self-explanatory. Adding the initial quantities owned by A and B, we obtain the total quantities of the two commodities as follows

$$\bar{x}_1 = \bar{x}_{A1} + \bar{x}_{B1}$$

and

$$\bar{x}_2 = \bar{x}_{A2} + \bar{x}_{B2}$$

We assume that the indifference curves† of A and B are convex to the origin, that is, that they have approximately the shape of the curves in figure 1.1. By taking the corresponding figure for consumer B, turning

---

† An indifference curve consists of all combinations of the two commodities between which the individual is indifferent. Thus, consumer A is indifferent to any two points on curve $I_A{}'$ in figure 1.1 and similarly for $I_A{}''$ and $I_A{}'''$. Moreover, A is assumed to prefer points above $I_A{}'$ to points on $I_A{}'$ so that for example points on $I_A{}''$ are preferred to points on $I_A{}'$ etc.

it upside down and combining it with figure 1.1 so that its axes pass through $\bar{x}_1$ and $\bar{x}_2$ in figure 1.1, we obtain the 'box diagram' of figure 1.2. The sides of the box equal the total initial quantities of the two commodities, $\bar{x}_1$ and $\bar{x}_2$. Point C inside the box denotes the initial distribution of the two commodities between A and B.

If A and B start trading with each other, they may reach a point such as D. This point implies a commodity distribution which both of them prefer to the original point C. (Point D is attained if A gives up $\bar{x}_{A2} - \bar{x}_{A2}^*$ and obtains $\bar{x}_{A1}^* - \bar{x}_{A1}^*$ in exchange.) All points inside the shaded area in figure 1.2 represent after-trade situations that both parties find

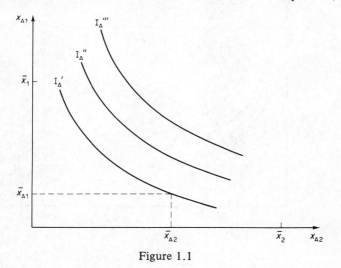

Figure 1.1

advantageous. A shift to such a point or to a point that A (or B) prefers, while B (or A) remains on his initial indifference curve (for example, points E and F), is said to fulfil the Pareto criterion. Moreover, for some of these points, such as D, E and F, further shifts preferred by both parties are impossible. Whenever this is true, we have reached a Pareto-optimal point, which means (as indicated a little while ago) that further shifts of the commodity distribution must make (at least) one party worse off.

Now, there are more Pareto-optimal points—or tangency points between two indifference curves, which amounts to the same thing—than D, E and F. In fact, there are Pareto-optimal points along a curve from the lower left-hand corner through EDF up to the upper right-hand corner of figure 1.2. Each point on this curve—a so-called contract curve—represents a particular (Pareto-optimal) distribution of welfare or 'real income' between the two consumers.

These distributions can be presented in a way that will be particularly useful later on. Let U_A and U_B on the axes of figure 1.3 express A's and B's *rankings* of various combinations of commodities†. All points not on the contract curve in figure 1.2 now become points inside the curve in figure 1.3, while points on the contract curve in figure 1.2—the set of

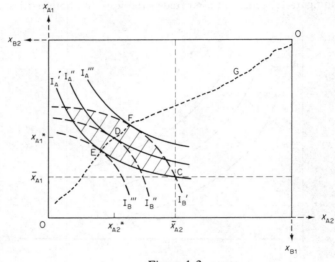

Figure 1.2

Pareto optima—correspond to points on the curve in figure 1.3, the so-called welfare frontier or utility-possibility curve (compare point C, which is not Pareto optimal and D, E, F and G which are).

To sum up the discussion thus far, we have established a criterion— the Pareto criterion—according to which it can be said that, for any given situation representable by a point outside the contract curve in figure 1.2 (such as C), there are better feasible alternatives represented by points on this curve (compare the segment E to F for C as the initial

---

† As U_A and U_B are rankings (or ordinal scales) only, actual distances between points on each axis have no particular meaning. The axes in figure 1.3 could, in other words, be stretched or shrunk without altering the required properties. See also appendix 1, section 1.1.

point). Given this criterion, a 'best' situation of commodity distribution in the economy—whatever is actually meant by 'best'—must occur some-where along the contract curve (or the welfare frontier), that is, it must be a Pareto optimum. Different points on the curve cannot be evaluated or ranked by the Pareto criterion, since movements along this curve imply that someone is made worse off. However, an individual observer or the government may subjectively rank the points on the contract curve and find that, say, D or G represents the best 'real income' distri-bution†.

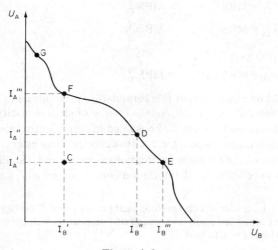

Figure 1.3

Given this background, economic theory has been confined to characterising the conditions that must be fulfilled in order to attain a Pareto-optimal allocation. It follows from what we have said that the condition for Pareto optimality in a barter economy—and, we may add, for a Pareto-optimal distribution of consumption in economies in general—

† We disregard the fact that certain points on the contract curve may be unfeasible in practice for institutional reasons or be so regarded. In these cases, the choice of a best welfare distribution may concern a point outside this curve. (Actually, when-ever such institutional constraints are present, the set of Pareto optima will be different; that is, the contract curve will have a different shape.) Nevertheless, one reason for neglecting such institutional constraints—which is essentially what we are going to do here—is that they may be questioned in the perspective we use here, that is from the viewpoint of social efficiency.

is that a tangency point between indifference curves be reached. This amounts to saying that the slopes of the indifference curves, the so-called marginal rate of substitution (MRS) between the two commodities, should be the same for both consumers. As this formulation is directly transferable to economies with more than two commodities and more than two consumers, we may state that the condition for Pareto-optimal (or efficient) consumption is *equality among marginal rates of substitution for each pair of commodities* $(1, 2, \ldots, M)$ and *for all consumers* $(A, B, \ldots N)$

$$\mathrm{MRS}_{12}^{A} = \mathrm{MRS}_{12}^{B} = \ldots = \mathrm{MRS}_{12}^{N}$$

$$\mathrm{MRS}_{13}^{A} = \mathrm{MRS}_{13}^{B} = \ldots = \mathrm{MRS}_{13}^{N} \qquad (1.1)$$

$$\ldots\ldots\ldots$$

$$\mathrm{MRS}_{1M}^{A} = \mathrm{MRS}_{1M}^{B} = \ldots = \mathrm{MRS}_{1M}^{N}$$

It should be observed that this formulation presupposes (a) that, in Pareto optima, all individuals consume some of all commodities and (b) that all commodities can be consumed in (sufficiently) divisible quantities (even cars, housing, etc.). However, nothing essentially new would be introduced if these assumptions were relaxed. (Similar reservations are also relevant for the optimum conditions presented below.)

Exercises   1. Show which feasible shifts from point C of figure 1.3 satisfy the Pareto criterion and which of these shifts will mean that a Pareto optimum is attained.

2. Explain why Pareto optimality does not prevail in a situation where A is indifferent between one additional unit of commodity 1 and two additional units of commodity 2 and where B is indifferent between two additional units of commodity 1 and one of commodity 2 (that is, where $\mathrm{MRS}_{12}^{A} = \frac{1}{2} \neq \mathrm{MRS}_{12}^{B} = \frac{2}{1} = 2$).

3. Try to question the general validity of the Pareto criterion as a value premise by explaining why point C in figures 1.2 or 1.3 can be regarded as superior to point E, assuming C and E are the only relevant alternatives.

1.2   A Production Economy (One Factor of Production)

Assume now that consumers supply producers with labour and that this constitutes the only factor of production. To keep the presentation simple, we assume to begin with that only one commodity (no. 1) is

produced. The consumer is assumed to have indifference curves with
respect to working time (or its opposite, leisure time) and commodity 1,
as shown in figure 1.4. (The shape of these curves indicates that more
labour requires more consumption in order for the individual consumer
to be indifferent to a change in the quantity of the two commodities.)

As labour can also be considered a commodity, even though it is
valued negatively in contrast to consumer goods, we may imagine an
exchange of labour and commodity 1 between two persons. Alternatively,
we may regard non-labour, that is leisure, as a positively valued commodity

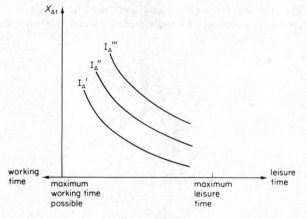

Figure 1.4

(see figure 1.4), exactly like commodity 2 above. We can therefore use
the approach presented in the preceding section to conclude that, in
Pareto optima, goods and leisure (F) or *goods and labour (P) should
be distributed so that the marginal rate of substitution between the two
is the same for all consumers*

$$MRS_{1F}^A = MRS_{1F}^B \ldots$$

or

$$MRS_{1P}^A = MRS_{1P}^B \ldots \qquad (1.2)$$

Let us assume that there are two firms producing commodity 1 with
decreasing returns from increased labour inputs. The marginal product
(MP) of labour, that is, the increase in production owing to an increase
of one unit of labour inputs, must now be the same for both producers,

I and II, for output of commodity 1 to be maximal (or efficient) for a
given total volume of labour input.

Exercise. Show why a situation in which the returns from the marginal
input of labour are two units of commodity 1 in company I and one unit
in company II cannot represent efficient use of a given amount of labour.

Thus an *efficient allocation of factors to producers is achieved when*

$$MP_{1P}^I = MP_{1P}^{II} = \ldots \tag{1.3}$$

Assume now that we are in a position where conditions (1.2) and (1.3)
are fulfilled and consumers are indifferent between one unit of commodity

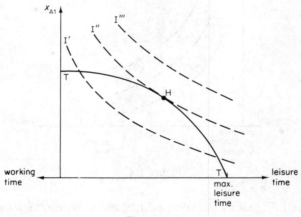

Figure 1.5

1 and one unit of labour (that is, $MRS_{1P}^i = 1; i = A, B, \ldots$), while the
marginal product of labour is two units of commodity 1 (that is, $MP_{1P}^j =
2; j = I, II, \ldots$). Under these circumstances, there are still feasible alterna-
tives that the consumers would prefer to the existing position. This
becomes evident if we let both consumers increase their supply of labour
by one unit and obtain the product thereof, that is two units of the
commodity. This obviously makes both consumers better off. As the
marginal product of labour *decreases* with increasing inputs and the
marginal rate of substitution *increases* with increasing labour supply
(that is, an increasing amount of commodity 1 is required to compensate for additional increases in labour supply; compare the increasingly

steeper slope of each indifference curve in figure 1.4), advantageous shifts of this kind may continue up to the point where

$$MRS_{1P}^{i} = MP_{1P}^{i} \tag{1.4}$$

In other words, condition (1.4) also has to be fulfilled in order to attain Pareto optimality.

The relevance of condition (1.4) can be illustrated in a simple fashion by assuming the existence of only one consumer and one producer. The TT-curve in figure 1.5 shows the producer's transformation of labour to commodity 1; the slope of the curve at each point (or each labour input) expresses the marginal product of labour, or the *marginal rate of transformation* between labour and commodity 1. At point H, where the marginal rate of substitution and the marginal rate of transformation coincide, that is, where condition (1.4) is fulfilled, the consumer reaches the highest possible indifference curve.

1.3   Production with Many Factors and of Many Goods

Let us assume that in addition to labour, allocated as indicated in the preceding section, there is a given set of machines (real capital) of uniform quality and that the returns from inputs of machinery are positive but decreasing. To attain a maximal output of commodity 1, these machines must be distributed between producers I and II so that their marginal products are identical in the two companies. If this occurs, we have a situation where both factors, labour and capital, are allocated in such a way as to make the marginal products the same in all (both) alternative uses. That efficiency requires an equality of this kind can be shown by analysing the allocation of resources between the two companies in the box diagram in figure 1.6. The curves in this diagram are isoquants (combinations of factors producing the same output) instead of indifference curves and the sides of the box now indicate the available amounts of the two factors. Reasoning similar to that used in the context of the previous box diagram (figure 1.2) can again be applied. We find that points outside the contract curve, that is points that are not points of tangency between isoquants and hence points where the marginal rates of transformation between factors differ, cannot be efficient: at each such point output in both companies can be increased†. (Verify this proposition.)

† The marginal rate of transformation between labour and machines means the incremental amount of labour required to keep output unchanged when machine

When both firms produce the same commodity, only *one* point on the contract curve will be efficient normally. In particular, when there are decreasing marginal returns to scale in both companies (that is, output grows by a decreasingly smaller amount when inputs of both factors are increased proportionately), there can be only one efficient point.

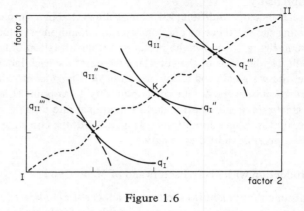

Figure 1.6

Exercise. Insert values of the isoquants in figure 1.6 to illustrate this conclusion.

If we now assume that companies I and II in figure 1.6 produce *different* commodities, points on the contract curve will again always be preferred to points outside the curve. In this case, however, we cannot *a priori,* that is without introducing consumer preferences, choose any particular point on this curve as an optimum point because a shift from one such point to another means that more of one commodity and less of another will be available. These options for society are portrayed in figure 1.7, where each point on the contract curve of figure 1.6 is represented by a point on the production possibility curve or transformation curve of this figure, that is by an efficient production point. (Compare the relationship between figures 1.6 and 1.7 and between figures 1.2 and 1.3; note that points outside the contract curve

input is reduced by one unit. (The term 'marginal rate of factor substitution' is not used here. By defining all production activities as 'transformations', regardless of whether a pair of commodities, a pair of factors or a factor–commodity pair is involved, important results can be formulated in simple terms; see for example page 12.

of figure 1.6 have their counterparts in points inside the transformation curve of figure 1.7. The shape of the curve in figure 1.7—concave to the origin—indicates that both companies are subject to decreasing marginal returns to scale.)

We have thus found a new condition for efficient allocation of resources, namely that *the marginal rate of transformation* (MRT) *between two factors must be the same for all companies* regardless of the type of commodities they produce

$$\text{MRT}^{\text{I}}_{P_1 P_2} = \text{MRT}^{\text{II}}_{P_1 P_2} \ldots \tag{1.5}$$

If we regard factors P_1 and P_2 as two kinds of human labour that are valued differently, such as physically strenuous work and some other

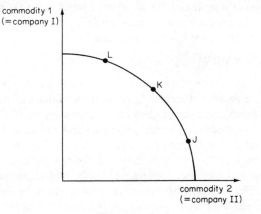

Figure 1.7

kind of labour, and if we assume that consumers can supply both kinds of labour, then, in line with the argument in the preceding section, the marginal rate of substitution between the two factors should be the same for all consumers in order to achieve a Pareto optimum, that is

$$\text{MRS}^{\text{A}}_{P_1 P_2} = \text{MRS}^{\text{B}}_{P_1 P_2} \ldots \tag{1.6}$$

and this uniform rate of substitution should equal the corresponding uniform rate of transformation

$$\text{MRS}^{i}_{P_1 P_2} = \text{MRT}^{j}_{P_1 P_2} \tag{1.7}$$

Exercise.   Investigate this proposition by analysing an assumption to the contrary as we have done in similar cases above.

Returning to figure 1.7, we may expect the slope of the transformation curve, that is the marginal rate of transformation between commodities 1 and 2, to have a certain relationship to condition (1.1), which concerned consumer substitution between the two commodities. This relationship can be established most easily by imagining that there is only one consumer. Introducing his indifference curves into figure 1.7, it is obvious that an optimum is reached at the point where the marginal rates of substitution and of transformation coincide, that is, where

$$\text{MRS}^{A}_{12} = \text{MRT}^{\text{total economy}}_{12} \tag{1.8}$$

This condition can easily be generalised to the case of more than one consumer.

To complete our discussion we should point out that whenever the companies can produce *both* commodities, it can be shown that the following equality must hold in optimum

$$\text{MRT}^{I}_{12} = \text{MRT}^{II}_{12} \tag{1.9}$$

We have now obtained a complete set of optimum conditions. If we had been able to draw diagrams in an arbitrary number of dimensions, we could have established the validity of the above conditions for an arbitrary number of commodities, factors, producers and consumers, instead of only a pair of each at a time. By using a mathematical, non-geometric mode of presentation, however, there are no impediments to showing that our conclusions can be generalised to the multidimensional, real-world case. The outcome of such a generalisation can be formulated as follows. *To attain a Pareto optimal (or efficient) allocation of factors and consumption* in an economy with decreasing returns to factors of production, with indifference curves of the shape used above (convex to the origin), with no external effects among producers and/or consumers (see section 2.1) and no collective goods (see section 2.2), *all marginal rates of substitution between relevant pairs of commodities, factors and commodity factors must be equal for all consumers. Moreover, the marginal rates of transformation must be equal for all producers concerned as well as equal to the corresponding marginal rates of substitution.* This formulation can be seen to be a verbal summary of conditions (1.1) to (1.9) presented above†.

---

† It should be observed that in an economy where collective goods and external effects are present, these conditions still hold, although the verbal formulation would be somewhat more elaborate. In such an economy, the conditions have to

1.4   A Market Economy

None of what has been said so far presupposes the existence of a *market* economy. In principle, a Pareto optimum, that is an allocation fulfilling conditions (1.1) to (1.9), is attainable with or without the use of a market mechanism. Our purpose in this section is to show that conditions (1.1) to (1.9) are fulfilled *automatically* in a particular system of markets in equilibrium called a perfect market economy. It should be pointed out that we are not in a position to demonstrate whether a perfect market economy can be said to fulfil these conditions in a more or less efficient way than other allocation systems such as various versions of a centrally planned economy. It may be added, however, that the economic litera-ture offers a number of arguments in favour of market systems, especially from the point of view of minimising the amount of information required in the economy.

Assume that the individual consumer is confronted with given market prices (p_i) and a given budget. Then, as is explained in detail in standard microeconomic theory‡, each consumer who tries to attain his highest possible indifference curve will in fact behave so that his marginal rate of substitution equals the corresponding relative prices, that is, for com-modities 1 and 2

$$\text{MRS}_{12}^{A} = P_2/P_1 = \text{MRS}_{12}^{B} \qquad\qquad (1.10)$$

Exercise.   Use the box diagram of figure 1.2 to show that a budget line can be drawn through point C and some point between E and F on the contract curve so that each consumer reaches a highest feasible indifference curve at the latter point, given the budget line! Explain the relationship between this point and expression (1.10).

Similarly, if we assume that consumers are able to adjust their supply of labour freely, their behaviour would lead to a situation which can be

---

refer explicitly to the marginal *social* rates of substitution and transformation (designating the relationships between the effects on all consumers and/or producers). These social rates could now deviate from the marginal *private* rates of substitution and transformation (designating the relationships between the effects solely on those who make the consumption and production decisions). Without collective goods and external effects these two concepts coincide.

‡ The reader is referred to any recent presentation of the elementary economic theory of household and company behaviour (see the bibliography at the end of the book).

defined simply by substituting labour (say, P_1) for commodity 2 in
expression (1.10).

Shifting to the production sector, companies producing both
commodities 1 and 2 can be expected to seek an output combination
at which the profit of each company is maximised. Illustrating this with
the transformation curve for each company at an optimum level of
factor inputs (see the curve TT in figure 1.8 for one of the companies)
we see that a point will be chosen where the highest profit line is
attained. (The profit lines V_1, V_2, etc. in figure 1.8 denote profit levels
in an increasing order; the slope of these lines is given by the relative

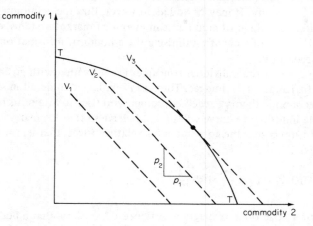

Figure 1.8

market prices for the two commodities.) Hence, the marginal rate of
transformation will equal the corresponding relative prices, that is

$$MRT^I_{12} = P_2/P_1 = MRT^{II}_{12} \tag{1.11}$$

From (1.10) and (1.11) it follows that $MRS^A_{12} = MRS^B_{12} = \ldots = MRT^I_{12} = MRT^{II}_{12} \ldots$ Since it can be shown in a similar way that the assumed
maximising behaviour of firms and consumers implies an equality be-
tween the remaining relevant pairs of substitution and transformation
rates, all conditions (1.1) to (1.9) for Pareto optimality will be fulfilled.

Exercise. Try to verify this proposition with respect to the substitution
and transformation rates for one commodity and labour in the case of
two consumers and two companies, when the companies produce only
this commodity and use only labour inputs.

However, a state of Pareto-optimal allocation cannot be achieved in just any market economy. Aside from the maximising behaviour of companies and consumers already postulated we have implicitly assumed (*a*) that the number of companies is variable, (*b*) that consumers and producers cannot affect market prices (that is, perfect competition prevails everywhere), (*c*) that all decision-makers are informed about current market prices and (*d*) that prices are formed so that all markets are simultaneously in equilibrium (that is, desired demand equals desired supply on all markets). (In chapter 2 we show how deviations from these assumptions lead to social inefficiency in an uncontrolled market economy and how such deviations may be corrected for by government intervention.)

Finally, it is important for the subsequent discussion to note that in a perfect market economy (a) market prices reflect the consumers' marginal valuations of each commodity, (b) the producers' marginal costs for a commodity reflect the amount of *other* commodities that must be sacrificed in order to produce an additional unit of the commodity in question and (c) Pareto-optimal allocation requires that the price on each market coincides with the producers' marginal costs. (See appendix 1 and page 137 in particular.)

1.5   An Intertemporal Economy

Up to this point we have considered an economy during a short period only and abstracted from the existence of a future beyond this single period. Hence there has been no need to observe the allocation of consumption and production over time and to take saving and investment aspects into account. In this section, we shall discuss the problem of allocation over time (intertemporal allocation) under some simplifying assumptions.

To start with, it should be pointed out that all the conclusions reached in the preceding sections remain valid in the intertemporal context. But these conclusions are now directly applicable only to part of consumer and producer activity. If we like, we may view the transition from an atemporal to an intertemporal economy in the following fashion. Producers have just realised that they can increase their output in the future by devoting part of their resources today to the production of capital goods to be used in a future period. Specifically, we may assume that the introduction of capital goods, produced from inputs of labour today, allows each given output of consumer goods in the next period to be produced by a smaller amount of labour than now. And if the future saving on labour inputs exceeds the labour input in today's capital goods production, these investments will have yielded a certain positive net return.

If, to continue this illustration, consumers show a willingness to trade consumer goods today for (larger quantities of) consumer goods tomorrow, it is also possible to free resources today for capital goods production. In an economy with one consumer, one producer and one consumer commodity, the intertemporal allocation problem may be described as in figure 1.9. The indifference curves of the consumer here refer to combinations of consumption today and consumption tomorrow. The transfor-

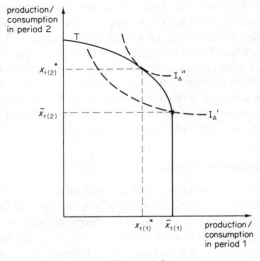

Figure 1.9

mation curve T shows feasible amounts of the consumer commodity in the two periods ($x_{t(1)}$ and $x_{t(2)}$, respectively).

Without any saving or investment, $\bar{x}_{t(1)}$ and $\bar{x}_{t(2)}$ of the consumer commodity would be produced and consumed in the two periods. This situation implies that the consumer reaches $I_A{}'$. Now, given that consumer goods production in period 1 can be reduced and that the resources thus made available can be used in capital goods production, the output of consumer goods in period 2 can be increased to such an extent that the consumer is more than compensated for the reduced consumption in period 1. To be specific, he would actually prefer to carry the reduction of $x_{t(1)}$ all the way down to $x_{t(1)}{}^*$ and receive the resulting increase of

$x_{t(2)}$ from $\bar{x}_{t(2)}$ to $x_{t(2)}*$; this shift would put him on the highest possible indifference curve.

Obviously this optimum position must have its counterpart in terms of an equality between some marginal rates of substitution and transformation. These rates can be seen to refer to consumer goods in period 1 and consumer goods in period 2 ($MRS_{t(1)t(2)} = MRT_{t(1)t(2)}$). On closer inspection, it can be seen that there is no difference in principle between on the one hand a particular commodity today and the 'same' commodity tomorrow and on the other two different commodities today. Thus we may easily accept the additional condition for Pareto optimal allocation that

$$MRS^{A}_{t(1)t(2)} = MRS^{B}_{t(1)t(2)} = \ldots = MRT^{I}_{t(1)t(2)} = MRT^{II}_{t(1)t(2)} \ldots$$

$$(1.12)$$

Exercise.   Try to formulate this condition verbally for an economy with only one type of consumer commodity.

Let us now introduce the concept of a *market economy* with many producers and consumers in the intertemporal context. Each consumer is assumed to be able to save at a certain market rate of interest. This provides him with an intertemporal budget line of the slope $1 + r$, departing from the initial position ($\bar{x}_{t(1)}, \bar{x}_{t(2)}$) as in figure 1.10. If the consumer now tries to attain his highest indifference curve, we end up in a position where the marginal rate of substitution equals the slope of the budget line; hence, the marginal rate of substitution will be the same for all consumers (who save). Similarly, profit-maximising producers who can borrow at the market interest rate will invest in capital goods up to the point where the marginal rate of transformation is made equal to $1 + r$, that is up to the point where the rate of return on marginal investments coincides with r. Under the assumption that the market rate of interest is determined in the same way as equilibrium prices on commodity markets, that is so that total demand (investment) is made equal to total supply (saving), we obtain a situation of general equilibrium *and* Pareto optimality since condition (1.12) is also fulfilled.

An extension of the market economy concept to include saving and investment activity thus allows Pareto optimality to be attained automatically in such an economy. The assumptions on which this economy now relies are, aside from those already mentioned in section 1.4, that the credit and capital goods markets must be in equilibrium, that prices of capital goods and interest rates are given for the individual decision maker and that there is perfect information about future markets and prices. In view of the severity of this final assumption, it should be added that a market economy can be shown to be capable of attaining Pareto-optimal positions also under more realistic conditions, that is for specific kinds of uncertainty about future prices.

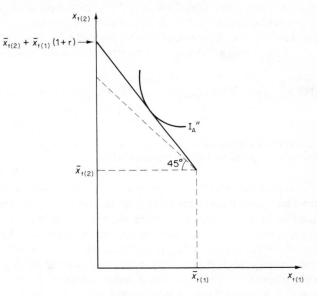

Figure 1.10

1.6 Summary

In this chapter, we have specified what conditions must be fulfilled in order to achieve social efficiency (Pareto optimality) in an economy. Moreover, we have seen that these conditions will be met automatically in a certain type of market system. This type of economy, the 'perfect market economy', is characterised by the absence of external effects, public goods and increasing returns and by the presence of general market equilibrium, a 'sufficient' degree of information and competition among many producers and many consumers.

2. IMPERFECTIONS AND THE NEED FOR ALLOCATION POLICY

Economic theory has been able to demonstrate that (a) under certain conditions, an economy with perfect competition on all markets has equilibrium positions (that is, situations where demand equals supply on every market), (b) every equilibrium position is socially efficient or Pareto optimal (that is, no individual can be better off without someone else being worse off) and (c) every conceivable Pareto-optimal situation (read: income distribution) corresponds to such an equilibrium position. This so-called perfect market economy constitutes the formal basis for propositions about the advantages of perfect competition. However, it is in no way intended as even an approximate description of reality. It nevertheless constitutes a practical analytical point of departure for discussing reality, that is to say, the implications of deviations from the conditions of the perfect market economy.

In the first part of this chapter we examine the implications of three essential deviations of this kind, which can be found in every existing economy. Our objective is to define these phenomena—external effects, public (or collective) goods and decreasing average costs — and then to see how the existence of such phenomena implies that the equilibrium positions of the economy cannot be Pareto optimal. Finally, examples are given of how the government can direct a market economy towards Pareto-optimal positions using economic policy instruments of various types.

Each of the three phenomena just mentioned can be said to involve a deviation from the *technical* assumptions behind the model of the perfect market economy, that is assumptions about production techniques and commodity properties. In the real world, there are also deviations from the *behavioural* assumptions behind the model. Two such behavioural imperfections involving obstacles to establishing and maintaining market equilibrium and competition among many traders are discussed in sections 2.5 and 2.6. Section 2.7 deals with a separate kind of deviation, imperfect *information*.

2.1   External Effects

2.1.1   Definitions and Examples

Efficiency in the allocation of resources and distribution of consumption in a market economy with perfect competition may be jeopardised if the actions of the individual producer or consumer affect not only himself but others as well. In general the individual decision maker will not take such side-effects, which may be quite extensive, into consideration. Hence the equilibrium positions of the uncorrected market economy will not fulfil the conditions for Pareto optimality.

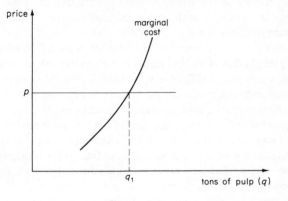

Figure 2.1

Effects of production on consumption   Pollution is the best-known example of these side-effects. A firm that releases waste products into the air or a river affects others who utilise these natural resources in some way. For example, consumers' satisfaction from utilising recreation areas may be reduced by air pollution. In cases such as this we say that there is a *negative (or detrimental) external effect* (or external diseconomy) on certain individuals' *consumption* as a result of certain *production* (for example, waste disposal from a pulp mill).

The situation may be illustrated as follows. If a pulp mill can sell its output at a given market price p, this price—in an otherwise perfect market economy—corresponds to the pulp consumers' valuation of the marginal increment of the commodity itself (see figure 2.1). In addition, there is a side-effect of the production process in the form of a negative external effect, the size of which is determined by the resulting reduction in the value of consumer services from recreation areas (forests, camping areas, etc.). For instance, we can assume that the value of these services decreases as the production of pulp increases. This is shown in figure 2.2, where v_1 represents the *decrease in value* corresponding to the various levels of production. Each additional ton of pulp means a reduction in value corresponding to what the consumer would have been willing to pay to avoid the marginal change. Here, the reduction in value diminishes as the production of pulp increases.

The total effect of pulp production on consumers of pulp and consumers of recreational facilities is represented by a vertical summation of the two curves p and v_1, where the reduction in value is denoted by a negative sign (see figure 2.3). Since the supply curve is assumed to reflect

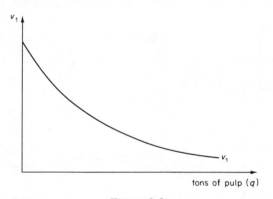

Figure 2.2

the firm's (and society's) costs in the sense of other goods sacrificed, the marginal costs at the quantity that maximises profit (q_1) will be greater than the total value of a marginal change in production. This situation is incompatible with a Pareto-optimal allocation of resources (see page 15 above).

Effects of production on other production   Fishermen's possibilities of making a given catch may also be reduced by the release of waste products into rivers, lakes or other waterways. In this case, the *production* of one commodity has a *negative external effect* on the *production* of another commodity. Given a certain production process in the firm producing pulp, the relationship between pulp production, water pollution, reduced supply of fish and reduced catch for fishermen can be determined in an analogous manner. Given the price of fish, a diagram

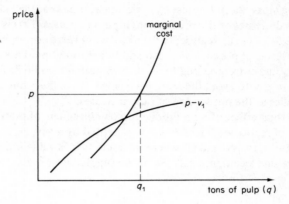

Figure 2.3

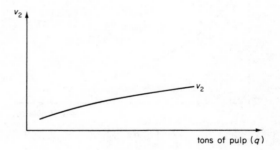

Figure 2.4

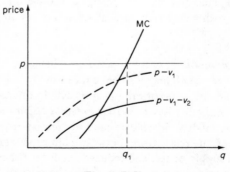

Figure 2.5

corresponding to figure 2.2 can be drawn, showing the effect of marginal
changes in pulp production on the value of fish production (v_2). We
assume in figure 2.4 that these effects are increasing in the relevant
interval. If this is the only external effect, the total value of the marginal
change in pulp production could be as shown in figure 2.3, except that the
$(p - v_1)$ curve would fall as production of pulp increases (figure 2.8). If
both of the external effects mentioned thus far occur simultaneously,
the corresponding curve will be as shown in figure 2.5. The difference
between society's marginal costs and the total of a marginal change in
production at the optimum level of production for the firm (q_1) is now
obviously greater than it was in figure 2.3.

Positive external effects (external economies) of production   External
effects of production are not necessarily negative. For example, if a
worker trained at the expense of one firm is employed at the same wage
by another firm where his training is of use, the second firm's production
has been positively affected by that of the first firm. Another example
would be that non-patented inventions such as new production processes
may also be utilised by firms other then the innovating firm and thus
represent a positive (or beneficial) external effect.

   In other cases positive and negative effects may exist simultaneously.
For example, smoke from oil refineries is favourable to the cultivation of
citrus fruit at the same time that it may have negative external effects
of the type mentioned earlier.

Exercise.   Draw the curve showing society's evaluation of different
amounts of production from an oil refinery with a given production
technique.

External effects of consumption   An individual's consumption may be
affected not only by the external effects of a company's production
but also by the consumption of other individuals. For example, an
individual may enjoy his neighbour's beautiful garden (positive external
effect of consumption) or he may be envious of his neighbour's beautiful
car (negative effect). If it cannot be assumed that the neighbour takes
these effects on outsiders into consideration (or if he should take them
into consideration by buying an even more impressive car), the distribution of consumption among individuals will not be optimal from
society's point of view. A less controversial example is how other peoples'
possession of a telephone increases the value of ones own possession of
a telephone.

In principle, we should calculate how much the individual affected would be willing to pay in order to obtain further positive external effects of other peoples' consumption and how much he would be willing to pay to have others reduce their consumption of the type that results in negative external effects. The total effect of the consumption of individuals could then be described in a way that would correspond to the earlier description of the total effect of production that gives rise to external effects. Figure 2.6 illustrates the case in which A's consumption of a certain commodity creates *negative* external effects whereby all consumers' valuation (S) of a marginal increment in A's consumption is less than A's valuation; that is, S lies under A's demand curve (D_A). Figure 2.7 shows a corresponding case where A's consumption gives rise to *positive* external effects[†].

2.1.2 Optimum Conditions and Economic Policy

External effects of consumption   The correct volume of consumption that gives rise to external effects is obtained when consumption is set at the level where society's valuation corresponds to price. Since the individual is assumed to behave in such a way that he increases his consumption as long as his own valuation of an additional unit exceeds the price,

---

† Formally, an external effect on an individual's consumption exists whenever his utility function includes not only variables under his own control (for example, x^A) but also variables that are controlled by other behaviour units (for example, x^B and q^{II}); for instance

$$U^A = F^A(x^A, x^B, q^{II})$$

where x^B is B's consumption and q^{II} is II's output.

An external effect on the output of a company exists whenever its production function includes not only variables under the control of the company itself (internal factors, such as L^I) but also variables controlled by other behaviour units (external factors, such as x^B and q^{II}); for instance

$$q^I = G^I(L^I, x^B, q^{II})$$

As is evident from these definitions, it is conceivable to have external effects of a consumption activity (for example, x^B) on a production activity (q^I). One example might be the effects of private automobiles—via increased congestion—on the output of transportation firms. However, this category seems to be much less significant than those discussed in more detail above.

It should be kept in mind that external effects in production and consumption, whenever they exist, must appear in the *production* and *utility functions,* respectively, as we have just indicated. Thus, the fact that the costs of a company are affected by other units' purchases or sales of factors of production, via the ensuing change in factor *prices,* does not constitute an external effect. The interdependence of units via the market mechanism is often called *pecuniary* 'external effects' or, perhaps less confusing, price effects.

the volume of consumption will be less than optimal under positive external effects and will exceed the optimum under negative effects.

Exercise.   Illustrate these propositions in figures 2.6 and 2.7.

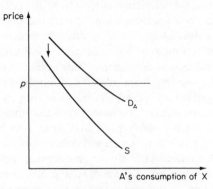

Figure 2.6   Negative effects of consumption

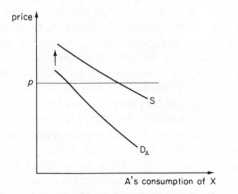

Figure 2.7   Positive effects of consumption

Society is naturally confronted with great difficulties if it attempts to steer consumption of different goods to their optimum levels. In the first place, measures would have to vary from one individual to the next and from one consumption commodity to another, and this would involve considerable administrative costs for economic policy. Since these costs must also be considered in determining an economically efficient distribution of goods and consumption, such detailed intervention can hardly be assumed to be justifiable.

In the second place, it is difficult, even in principle, to identify and measure external effects of consumption in a satisfactory way. Furthermore it may be reasonable to assume that such external effects, although they have been widely discussed, are often not of very great importance in the sense that those individuals subjected to the external effects would not be willing to pay a significant sum to have the situation corrected. Also it should be noted that it is often difficult to determine whether these external effects are positive or negative. 'Status-oriented' consumption may be mentioned as an example. This usually means that an individual suffers in some way from others' consumption of a certain commodity (negative external effect) and therefore also feels compelled to consume the commodity. The observation that the consumption of a certain commodity has grown rapidly in a region may be explained equally well by the fact that consumers obtain *information* about the existence and characteristics of the commodity through others' consumption. As long as the individual is assumed to prefer more information to less, this external effect must be regarded as positive rather than negative.

So far we have dealt with aspects that reduce the need for economic policy to make corrections for external effects of consumption. There are, however, cases in which external effects can be assumed to be unambiguous, significant and, moreover, approximately equal for all consumers in a country or region. In these cases, a correction would appear to be simpler and therefore advisable. For example, acquisition of a telephone could be subsidised in view of its positive external effects, or a general fee or tax (such as the petrol tax) could be levied on the use of automobiles in view of congestion and the resulting negative external effects on other motorists. In some cases, similar measures may be more adequately taken at a municipal or some other regional level. The way in which these kinds of taxes and subsidies correct the distribution of consumption will become apparent below.

External effects of production   External effects of production on *consumption* are often, of course, as difficult to measure as the effects of consumption on other peoples' consumption (compare the example concerning the external effects of production on consumption of recreational services). However, it should be emphasised that measurement difficulties are not sufficient reason for refraining from corrective action. In many cases it is quite obvious that something must be done even if the exact nature of the measures have to be determined arbitrarily.

In some cases at least the order of magnitude of the external effects on consumption can be estimated rather accurately.

Since it is often easier to calculate the extent of external effects in the case of effects of production on *production* (as in the fishing example above), let us take a case of this kind as the point of departure for a more rigorous presentation of optimum conditions and economic policy measures.

Assume, as was done in figure 2.4, that a certain known *negative* external effect (v_2) arises from the production of an amount of commodity, q. Figure 2.8 shows that the socially optimal level of production, q_0, where society's total valuation of marginal changes in production is

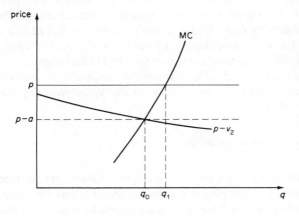

Figure 2.8

equal to marginal cost (MC), is less than the optimum of production for the company, q_1. Now, there are several possible means of correcting the production level in order to fulfil the condition for an optimum, that is that $MC = p - v_2$.

(1) The firm may be taken over into public ownership and operated so that the total effects on the economy are given due consideration.

(2) If the number of parties concerned is small, direct settlement among these parties may be arrived at, possibly on the initiative of and through the mediation of the government.

(3) The private firm may be prohibited from producing more than q_0.

(4) The firm may be required to pay a fee corresponding to the negative external effect. This fourth and least self-evident measure will now be analysed more closely.

Ideally the fee should be flexible and designed in such a way that the total amount paid by the firm equals the value of the total external effect for any value of q. Then the company's net revenue would be described by $p - v_2$, and the adjustment would take place with respect to this curve instead of p. This would result in production q_0[†].

In practice we may have to be satisfied with charging a unit fee a which approximately corresponds to the size of the marginal external effect *in the optimal situation* (q_0) and apply this fee generally. The company's net price curve would then be $p - a$, as indicated by the broken line in figure 2.8. The optimum for the company is then the same as for society (q_0). It should be noted that it is easier to calculate and administer a uniform fee of this kind, but that precision in this method requires a change in the fee as soon as price or marginal cost changes.

Similarly, we can show how *positive* external effects can be corrected. In this case, method (4) prescribes a *subsidy* to the company that creates the external effects.

Exercise.   Draw this diagram.

The effects of economic policy corrections   One of the consequences of the method of charging fees described above is that the company's output with given methods of production will be adjusted to the optimal level because the company also has to pay for the use of 'external factors of production' such as water, air, etc. Thus enterprises will stop using these factors of production uneconomically, whereas there would otherwise be no incentive to do so. In addition, these measures lead to favourable effects in the long term.

First of all, if several possible processes are known, the production process will be changed so that less of the 'factors of production' that have risen in price (from zero to the level of the fee) will be used. In other words, there will be an adjustment similar to the one that occurs when the price of labour rises relative to other factors.

[†] As an alternative to the diagrammatical technique used so far, the negative external effects could be added to the marginal cost curve so that the sum would equal 'total social marginal costs'. Analogously the fees could be added to the company's other marginal costs, instead of being subtracted from the price.

Secondly, research activity will now concentrate on developing new methods of production aimed at economising on the now more expensive factor of production. An example of this is the development of purification facilities for the firm's waste products. In all these cases it is assumed that the fees will be adjusted to correspond to the reduced level of pollution achieved. This will occur automatically if the fees are based on the amount of harmful materials released rather than the quantity of output produced.

The regulation method (3) can be used to achieve almost the same results in terms of affecting incentives to reduce negative external effects if it can be made flexible enough and, in particular, if it is the amount of effluents rather than the amount of output that is regulated. But if flexibility is low, incentives will be ineffectual or absent; the company's interest in adjusting production methods and developing new ones diminishes, of course, if the volume of production is not allowed to increase. In addition and in contrast to the charging of fees, it is often difficult in practice to use the regulation method so that firms are dealt with according to the size of their respective negative external effects and costs of reducing these effects. In this sense the regulation method is less efficient in the short as well as the long term.

For negative external effects of the water pollution type, there is a special kind of measure option in addition to the four mentioned above, namely connection to a central purification or destruction plant. The connection may be established either through a sewage system or through conventional transport (of poisonous materials). Obviously, the use of this alternative depends on the costs of connection and purification. It can be shown that this solution, even if it means that all negative effects will cease and even if the costs of purification are less than the tax the firm would otherwise pay, is not always suitable from the economic point of view of society. In figure 2.9 the same company as in figure 2.8 is indicated. The area ABC can under certain conditions be regarded as an expression of the company's social surplus in the presence of the fee a; that is to say, ABC represents the difference between society's total valuation of production minus total costs. If the company can be connected to a central purification plan with a purification cost of r per unit produced, the optimal level of production will be q_2, total costs (including purification) will be equal to the area under the MC $+ r$ curve and therefore the social surplus at complete purification will be the area A′ B′ C′. It is apparent for the particular case shown in the figure that the social surplus is less than it would be if fees were charged instead

(ABC), despite continuation of pollution to a certain degree in the latter case. We may also note that the difference between the two alternatives would have been even greater if we had taken the costs associated with establishing the purification connection into account.

The conclusion is that given the costs for connection the purification costs must be lower than a certain value, possibly far below the fee *a*, if purification is to be preferred from society's viewpoint. This example illustrates how it may be socially warranted to *reduce* pollution, but not *eliminate* it.

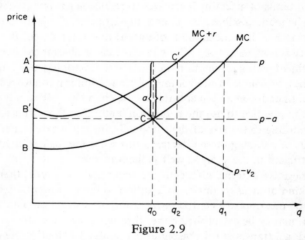

Figure 2.9

Distribution and compensation problems Up to now we have discussed pure efficiency aspects of external effects. There is also a 'welfare distribution aspect'. Forcing the company to adjust in the way indicated will not eliminate completely the negative external effects except in special cases. These cases arise (with the exception of the purification case just mentioned) when the external effects are so large that the regulated production volume is set at zero, or, alternatively, when the fee is set so high that continued production using production methods that give rise to pollution is no longer profitable.

In the cases where external effects remain, although at an optimal level (that is, where costs of further reductions exceed benefits), the party subjected to these effects will continue to be affected. This is where a compensation problem arises. (A possible exception is method 2 above involving direct settlement between the parties concerned.) A crucial question in this context is under what circumstances did the external effects first appear. For example, if the water- or air-polluting company were established before the fisheries and recreation areas, compensation to fishermen, etc. may be regarded as unjustified. The latter would rather experience an 'unearned' advantage from the decrease in the polluting company's production.

On the other hand, if the external effects appeared *later* than the affected activities, compensation may be considered justifiable. When fees are charged, the receipts from the fees can be transferred to the affected party. It should be observed that the total fees, determined as above on the basis of *marginal* external effects in the optimal equilibrium situation (= area between p and $p - a$), is not equal to the total size of the external effects (= area between p and $p - v_2$), which determines the amount of compensation. If the marginal negative external effects are decreasing as in figure 2.2, then the yield from the fees will not suffice to cover the compensation payments; in the opposite case, less than the total yield will be required for the payments (see figure 2.8).

The valuations of society versus the valuations of individuals   Up to now we have only considered the 'welfare' of generations now living when determining corrective measures. Several kinds of external effects are cumulative in the sense that each new increment is permanent or at least extends far into the future. In this case society may feel it has a duty to attempt to care for the interests of *future generations* and to take measures other than those discussed thus far.

In addition, society, through government and parliament, may have so-called *merit wants,* that is values that differ from those of individuals. For example, this is why society subsidises cultural activities, athletics and the like, while it taxes and regulates the use of alcohol and other stimulants. Similarly, society might want to stimulate basic research (which has positive external effects) and prevent pollution more than may be assumed to be consistent with the citizens' (conscious?) interests. This may take place by making fees and subsidies higher than indicated in our previous discussion. Furthermore, the government may take measures in order to restore a previous state of the environment to the greatest possible extent or to 'clean up' after continued pollution, which we saw above may be reasonably accepted. However, it is incorrect that, as has sometimes been asserted, the government should use exactly the amounts of receipts yielded by pollution fees for this purpose. A 'merit want' can lead to government measures that cost *more or less* than these yields.

2.1.3   Summary

External effects are side-effects of consumption or production activities
on the consumption or production activities of others that the party
responsible does not take into account. As no attention is paid to these
side-effects in the market economy, the government must intervene with
taxes and subsidies, regulation or other corrective measures in order to
attain social efficiency. Briefly stated, the criterion is that social rather
than private marginal revenues and marginal costs should be equalised.
This implies that the activity that creates negative (positive) external
effects should be reduced (increased). In the socially optimal position
negative effects will generally persist to some extent.

2.2   Public Goods

The goods that are considered in the theory of the perfect economy are
characterised by the property that each unit can be consumed by one
consumer only (so-called private goods). In reality, there are also goods
which simultaneously satisfy several consumers; that is to say, the
addition of another consumer does not reduce the quantity consumed
by others. These goods are called collective or public goods. Examples
are services provided by national defence, the legal system, fire service,
streets, radio transmission, action against insects that spread disease and
the like. As there are by definition no costs involved in serving additional
consumers, a price should not be charged for these services. But with a
zero price and non-zero production costs, output cannot be determined
in the usual way by market demand and market supply.

2.2.1   Optimum Conditions

In principle the demand for a public good can be determined in the
following way. Just as we assumed in general for private goods, the individual consumer can assign a money value to the marginal increment of
a public good as indicated in figure 2.10. In other words, if a price were
charged for this service, the individual's demand curve would have the
appearance indicated. The principal difference as compared with private
goods, however, arises in the determination of the *total* demand. Since
a public good is, by definition, a good that can be consumed by one
individual without reducing other individuals' possibilities of consuming
it (for example, radio programmes), the total demand is calculated as a

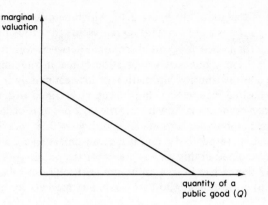

Figure 2.10

vertical summation of the individual demand curves. (The demand curve for a private good where the consumption of one individual leaves less for others at a given supply, is calculated by *horizontal* summation of the individual demand curves.) The total demand for a public good in an economy with two consumers is illustrated in figure 2.11.

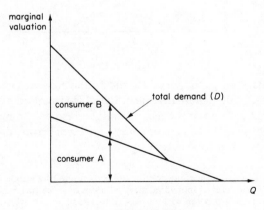

Figure 2.11

If the total demand for a given public good is known, the socially efficient output of the good occurs when the marginal cost for producing the good is equal to the sum of all the individual valuations of a marginal increment of the good[†]. In figure 2.12, which describes a special case in which marginal costs are constant, $\bar{Q}$ represents the efficient output.

How the total costs for $\bar{Q}$ are distributed between consumers is not a matter of efficiency but purely a question of real income distribution. One particular distribution alternative, of interest mainly in those cases where the desired income distribution can be attained with specific means, deserves mention, however. If the cost per unit of the public good is distributed among the consumers according to their marginal valuations at $\bar{Q}$, P_A and P_B, respectively, and if the consumers regard the fees for the good calculated in this way as prices for the public good, they will clearly find themselves in an equilibrium position (a so-called pseudo-equilibrium) corresponding to that existing in markets for private goods.

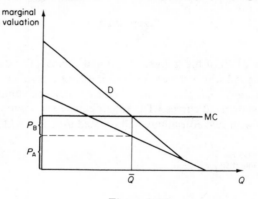

Figure 2.12

In other words, with given 'prices' P_A and P_B the consumers prefer quantity $\bar{Q}$ to all other alternative quantities. (This method of charging also means that the sum of the fees per unit corresponds to marginal cost; and, in this particular case of constant marginal costs, the total receipts exactly cover total costs.)

---

† Formally, the optimum condition for the production of a public good is equality between the sum of individual marginal rates of substitution, and the marginal rate of transformation with respect to this good and an arbitrary private good. This means, using the symbols of chapter 1, that

$$\mathrm{MRS}\,_{1k}^{A} + \mathrm{MRS}\,_{1k}^{B} = \mathrm{MRT}_{1k}$$

where commodity 1 is a private good and k denotes the public good. Compare the corresponding condition for two private goods

$$\mathrm{MRS}\,_{12}^{A} = \mathrm{MRS}\,_{12}^{B} = \mathrm{MRT}_{12}$$

We have seen that, under the assumption that the individuals' valuations of public goods are known, the existence of such goods does not lead to any complicated analytical problems. The real difficulty is related to the realism of the assumption that consumer valuations of the public good are known or can be ascertained.

2.2.2   Determination of Demand for Public Goods

If the government, in an attempt to achieve an efficient volume of production of a public good along with a distribution of payments as indicated above, asks consumers how much they are willing to pay for marginal changes in production, there are great risks that the answers will be consciously distorted. If the individual consumer understands than an increase in production will not cause him to pay any noticeable increase in taxes or a special fee, he may tend to answer with an *exaggerated* demand for the public good relative to his true demand. (Such an understanding can exist, for example, in general statements or simple interview studies concerning desires for better roads, increased police protection and the like.) On the other hand, if the individual knows that he will really have to pay in accordance with his expressed willingness to pay (compare figure 2.12) and, moreover, that he is one of a great many consumers, he knows that he has complete control over how much he himself will have to pay but that he has meagre possibilities for affecting the *total* demand. In this situation he may attempt to take advantage of the expressed willingness to pay of others and indicate a low willingness to pay (the so-called 'free-rider problem'). Thus a tendency to *understate* the true willingness to pay for public goods would arise.

It has been shown theoretically that the problem of getting consumers to reveal their true valuations is solvable only in certain special situations. In the absence of a general solution, 'informed guesses' by the political representatives of the people have to serve as the basis for decisions about the volume and distribution of payments for public goods[†].

2.2.3   Transformation of Public Goods into Marketable Goods

There is hardly any case in which a public good *must* be delivered at zero price. A public good can be transformed into a marketable good (to be

---

[†] It is often argued that this tends to lead to an undersupply of public goods (see, for example, Galbraith, *The Affluent Society,* and Downs, 'Why the Government Budget is too small in a Democracy', in *Private Wants and Public Needs,* ed. E. Phelps). In principle the opposite tendency is also conceivable.

produced and sold by a public *or* private enterprise) through different
more or less expensive mechanisms of distribution. In other words, a
public good may be transformed into a good from which the non-paying
consumer is excluded. For example, as is well known, there are instances
where a non-zero price (toll) is charged for the utilisation of certain
uncongested roads—a public good. In other cases, there are technical
possibilities for achieving such a transformation, but for reasons such as
cost these possibilities have not been exploited. This applies, for example,
to 'Pay TV', where it is technically possible to allow only those who pay
for a certain programme to watch it on their receivers.

The advantage of excluding those who do not pay for access to a
public good is that the problem of determining total demand is eliminated
or is at least considerably reduced. The disadvantage is, of course, that
a price is introduced in spite of the fact that the marginal cost of adding
another consumer (automobile driver or TV-viewer) is zero, and this in
itself implies inefficient resource allocation. In other words, in each
separate case this disadvantage as well as the cost of charging a price
has to be weighed against the advantages of gaining information about
the total demand for the good.

2.2.4   Summary

Public goods (collective goods) are goods that can be consumed by
several consumers simultaneously in such a way that the consumption
of one individual does not decrease another's possibility of consuming
the same good. The Pareto-optimal volume of a public good is obtained
(in an otherwise perfect economy) where the sum of consumer valuations
of a marginal increment is equal to the marginal cost of producing the
good. The main problem of achieving this volume in practice is that it is
difficult to ascertain the true demand (willingness to pay).

2.3   Decreasing Cost Industries (Economies of Scale)

The assumption of perfect competition is based on the understanding
that there is a large number of companies producing a certain good with
rising average variable costs in the short term (rising average total costs
for each company in the long term). At the opposite extreme, there are
in reality sectors where *one* firm has the lowest feasible average costs and
operates in an interval of production where average costs are decreasing
(see figure 2.13). It is sometimes said that economies of scale exist in

such a sector. Familiar examples include regional telephone, postal and railway services.

2.3.1   The Pricing Problem

If a company producing under decreasing cost conditions exploits its monopoly position and maximises profits, that is, produces where marginal cost (MC) equals marginal revenue (MR), the price would exceed and the production volume be less than the socially efficient values. A socially efficient price–quantity combination is obtained where price equals marginal cost (see q_e); in other words, production should be increased as long as the market value (price) is greater than marginal cost (see page 15).

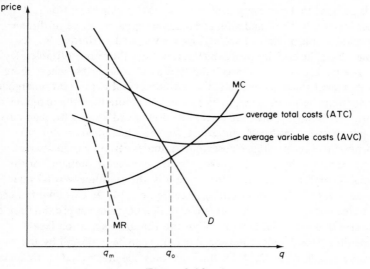

Figure 2.13

The main problem with the marginal cost pricing principle whenever there are economies of scale is that the company will thereby operate at a loss (see figure 2.13). We have thus changed the company's output from q_m, where a profit is obtained, to q_o, which is better from a social point of view but which involves a financial deficit. This means, of course, that a *private* firm cannot be made to operate at the desired level of production without being allowed to collect a 'licence fee' as

well (giving rise to two-part tariffs well-known from the public utilities
sector) or without receiving a subsidy from the government sufficient
to cover the resulting financial deficit. An alternative solution is for
the government to take over production, a solution that has been
employed in many cases of this nature.

We have thus indicated how price and output should be determined
and how production can be organised in an otherwise perfect economy,
if there are decreasing average costs in a sector where some positive level
of production is to take place. Whether any production at all is in the
interest of society remains to be determined.

2.3.2   The Investment Criterion

It is obvious that not every case in which the pricing condition just
mentioned is fulfilled and a financial deficit appears can be profitable
from the point of view of society. Hence we need a criterion for dis-
tinguishing the socially profitable sectors from the non-profitable.

The reason why social profitability is at all conceivable where there is
a permanent financial deficit is that consumers value their intramarginal
units (units between O and q_o in figure 2.14) more than the marginal
unit, that is, higher than the price. The downward sloping demand curve
is an expression, although imperfect, for this phenomenon. For our
purpose here let us simply observe that, under certain circumstances,
the area under the demand curve provides an exact expression for the
social 'benefit side' of the industry, that is, the consumers' total valuation
of the *whole* volume of output q_o (see figure 2.14). In certain other cases
the area under the demand curve is a sufficiently close approximation of
the size of total social benefits. With this general reservation (see
appendix 2 for details) total social benefits can be indicated by the
shaded area in figure 2.14. Of this area, only the area pCq_oO is financial
revenue. The relevant level of total costs can be derived from the average
total cost (ATC) curve; they are equal to the area ABq_oO. The criterion
for deciding whether production is socially profitable or not is therefore
that social benefits should be greater than total costs, that is to say,
$ECq_oO > ABq_oO$ or EDA > DBC. (It should be apparent from the
demand and marginal cost curves in the figure that the pricing criterion
discussed above maximises the difference between social benefits and
costs.)

In the case illustrated in figure 2.14 the investment criterion is
obviously fulfilled, which means that production of this good can be

said to be socially profitable. Observe that in this case (in contrast to the case in figure 2.13) a financial surplus is not possible at any volume of production; in other words, the strict market economy would not have resulted in any production of this good at all.

To take an example, let us assume that figure 2.14 describes a neighbourhood shop whose services (q) were previously demanded according to the D'' curve but now only to the extent shown by the D' curve. The shop cannot survive in the present situation even if it were to adopt a monopolistic pricing policy. Our presentation of this situation indicates,

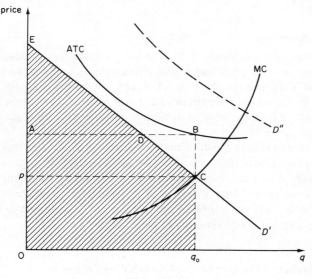

Figure 2.14

however, that the customers value the services of the shop so highly that the total costs are covered by their maximum willingness to pay. By encouraging cooperative actions among consumers or by introducing subsidies, the government might help to keep such local service units alive. (It should be observed, however, that the latter type of intervention would imply an income redistribution from taxpayers in general to the consumers concerned.)

The application of the investment criterion is complicated by the fact that more than one or two points on the demand curve are very seldom known. In other words, it is difficult to estimate consumers' total valuation of q_0 in practice. However, some guidance can often be obtained if it is known that production gives a financial surplus at some volume of production (for example q_m in figure 2.13). If this is so the volume q_o which has been shown to be superior to any positive level of output must also be socially profitable.

The use of these criteria may be further complicated in practice since it may be difficult to raise the government revenue needed to cover the financial deficit at the efficient level of production without causing inefficiency in some other part of the economy. For example, it can be shown that most types of taxes have such a distorting effect (see chapter 3).

2.3.3 Summary

For sectors of the economy with decreasing average costs, social efficiency in production under ideal circumstances would mean operating at a loss. That railways, the post office, etc., show losses may (to the extent that these cases represent such a cost situation) be compatible with social efficiency, while showing a profit under the same assumptions would not be.

In order to decide which of the productive activities with financial losses are profitable from a social viewpoint a relatively complicated investment criterion is required which would comprise an attempt to measure consumers' total valuation of the volume of production, that is how much they are willing to pay in order not to be forced to do entirely without the commodity in question.

2.4   Technical Imperfections—A Concluding Comment

In the preceding three sections we have seen that a strict market economy is incapable of reaching an equilibrium that is Pareto optimal, since it is unable to take external effects into account, produce public goods and supply an optimal quantity of goods produced under decreasing costs. In all three cases the absence of a satisfactory market mechanism necessitates economic policy measures (if Pareto optimality is desired). These three types of market imperfection have the common characteristic that determining the nature and extent of the economic policy measures required raises complicated measurement problems and involves heavy informational requirements especially regarding consumers' willingness to pay. In other words, these imperfections give rise to problems and requirements that are practically non-existent in the perfect economy where no one needs to know anything about the rest of the world except the various market prices.

In all the market imperfections dealt with we have seen that pricing and investment problems arise. For example, how should the net price for firms creating external effects be determined and when should society invest in purification plants; to what extent should public goods be produced and how should 'the price' be distributed among consumers; how should the size of the plant and price be determined under economies of scale?

We have also observed that for all three deviations from the perfect economy, economic policy corrections often create needs for (increased) government income to subsidise positive external effects, to finance the production of public goods and to cover financial losses in sectors with decreasing average costs. Since it is very difficult in practice to raise such revenue without disturbing the operation of the economy in other respects, this often becomes a question of weighing different types of social inefficiency (see chapter 3).

We now turn from the technical imperfections to discuss the effects of certain *behavioural* imperfections, that is, deviations from the behaviour assumptions behind the perfect market economy model.

2.5   Market Disequilibrium

The concepts of a perfect market economy and perfect competition require the assumption that prices everywhere are adjusted to bring demand and supply into equilibrium. This property is obviously of great value to those who trade on the markets, since a situation of *excess demand* would imply that the consumers' demand is not satisfied at the going price and a situation of *excess supply* that all producers cannot sell the amount they would like to sell at the given market price.

Exercise.   Use a diagram to illustrate these two situations and indicate what factors determine the size of excess demand and excess supply, respectively.

Of the two kinds of market disequilibrium mentioned excess supply is of more limited interest. It is unusual for a price at which supply exceeds demand to persist except for a short period of time. In order to increase sales towards the desired level, producers can sooner or later be expected to lower their prices, possibly by introducing discounts of one kind or another. In other cases the 'adjustment' may take the form of government intervention by which a high price level is supported by government purchases to clear the market (for example, agricultural policy schemes in many countries)[†].

It is more interesting then to observe the case of a market left in a state of excess *demand*. The main reason why situations of this kind arise is perhaps the existence of government price regulation such as rent regulation or the more widespread regulation of interest rates. There are, however, examples of 'private' price regulations as well; a case in point is the pricing agreement among the world's leading copper exporters in the mid-1960s. Although our main objective in this chapter is to elucidate the inefficiency of the uncontrolled market economy, it seems more relevant to depart from this theme in the present section and to take examples from the permanent disequilibrium situations created by government intervention.

2.5.1 Welfare Implications of a Permanent Excess Demand

Let us consider the market for a certain commodity, say, housing in a given area. For simplicity, we disregard for a moment the fact that housing units differ in size and quality. In figure 2.15 $\bar{S}$ represents the given supply and D indicates the demand for housing at various rent levels. If the authorities set the rent level at $\bar{p}$, that is, at a level below the equilibrium rent, p_0, a situation arises where demand exceeds supply. (The size of the resulting excess demand is shown by ED in the figure.) This means, first of all, that the rent no longer works as an equilibrating allocation mechanism and that the market is locked in a position of *unsatisfied demand*[‡].

The consumers who are forced away from the market due to their

---

† There are exceptions when excess supply disequilibria are both permanent and important. One example is provided by the labour market in the presence of effective *minimum wages* by which the equilibrium wage level for certain groups of employees will be exceeded. Hence, a state of permanent excess supply (unemployment) will emerge in the affected segment of the labour market. (See also footnote page 77.)

‡ This implies that the consumer's marginal rate of substitution between a regulated commodity 1 and an unregulated commodity 2 (both considered as divisible commodities; see page 6) cannot be made equal to the relative prices, that is $MRS^i_{21} \neq p_1/p_2$. It is this fact that makes it impossible to have the Pareto-optimum conditions fulfilled in the presence of excess demand on a market (see section 1.4).

inability to find housing at the going price will have to use their incomes
for something else, which they obviously do not find equally attractive,
for example, more expensive cars.

Secondly, the given supply is not likely to be distributed among those
who have the highest valuations of the commodity, that is among those
who, due to high incomes and/or strong preferences for the commodity,
are willing to pay the most to obtain it. Assuming, for example, that
there are q_0 households competing for the $\bar{S}$ units of housing ($q_0 > \bar{S}$),
a household with a low valuation of housing (for example, A in figure 2.15)
may succeed in getting hold of a flat whereas another with a much

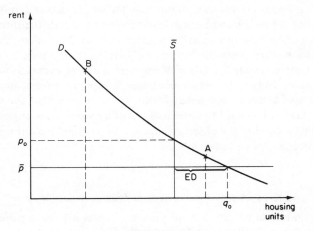

Figure 2.15

higher valuation does not (for example, B in the figure). Hence, we end
up with an *inefficient distribution of consumption* in the sense that a
household, in spite of the fact that it values renting a flat more (that
is, is willing to pay more), has to relinquish it to another household.
(We return to this aspect in section 2.5.2 below.)

Thirdly, price regulation stimulates the emergence of a black market.
Such a market has at least two kinds of negative effect. (a) The share
of the supply sold on the black market will carry a price equal to the
equilibrium price p_0, perhaps more. This implies that for the market as
a whole *different consumers will be charged different prices for the
same commodity*. (b) Efforts to conceal transactions on the black
market (by avoiding advertising, etc.) as well as the possible efforts on

the part of the authorities to put a stop to this illegal activity will have the effect of making *transactions* on the market as a whole *more resource consuming*.

In connection with this cost aspect, a fourth effect of price regulation should be mentioned, that is that *costs of rationing* in terms of queueing, etc., will arise on the legal side of the market. This is another way of saying that the simple allocation mechanism provided by an equilibrating price is replaced by a more complicated method of allocation, 'rationing'.

Over and above these four effects there are negative effects on the supply side as well. First of all, the price regulation implies that production normally falls short of what it would have been at the equilibrium price p_o†. Furthermore, it is *hard to estimate the size of demand* in the presence of a price below the equilibrium level; therefore, it is difficult to determine the size of construction activity required to clear the market. Typically, some consumers queue up 'just in case', while others believe it to be 'meaningless' to join the queue when there is a large excess demand on the market. Hence, the observable queue is likely to present an incorrect estimate of actual excess demand; and, what is even worse, the *direction* of the bias will be hard to determine. In other words, it is impossible to determine whether the observable queue for housing over- or under-estimates the true housing shortage.

2.5.2   Motives for and Alternatives to Price Regulation

A typical reason for government price regulation is to keep consumer outlays for an 'indispensable' commodity at a low level. Or, the purpose may be to reduce consumption expenditure in general for certain groups of consumers and in particular perhaps, for low-income households. The motives behind objectives of this kind are either a disapproval of consumer preferences (see the discussion of merit wants on page 31 above) or a desire to redistribute real income in society. With respect to the first motive—the government's belief that people in general ought to

---

† With respect to housing supply, the following solution has been used in some countries: Rents for new flats are based on actual production costs. This in turn leads to a new set of problems owing to the rent differences between new and old flats, even when consumers regard flats of both types as equally valuable. This pricing principle also tends to eliminate incentives for cost reductions in the construction industry, since the actual costs of production are accepted as a basis for pricing and it is often possible—due to the excess demand—to find tenants even for new and very expensive housing.

consume more of the regulated commodity—price regulation, resulting as it does in excess demand, is clearly inadequate. As we have seen, it is demand only, and not supply, that is increased by keeping prices low. Thus regulating prices below the equilibrium level, we typically end up with a reduction, rather than an expansion, of actual consumption.

Considering now the income redistribution motive we find again that price regulation is far from an ideal instrument. A situation of excess demand implies that some consumers cannot benefit from the low, regulated price level; some manage to get only little or perhaps nothing at all of the commodity. And among the consumers in this category there will, of course, be some whom the government wanted to support by means of the regulated price. In fact, it is often precisely those whose real income the government intends to increase who are left with a particularly small share of the commodity. The low-income family, for example, often lacks the kind of experience or education and the necessary contacts that facilitate access to the inadequate supply of a regulated commodity.

Turning to possible alternative policies to price regulation, we may note first of all that a desired income redistribution is more easily achieved by a direct money transfer to the group concerned. If, instead, the objective is to encourage consumption of a particular commodity (*merit wants*), this can be attained not by regulating the price below the equilibrium level, as already pointed out, but by subsidising the commodity and, at the same time, maintaining equilibrium between supply and demand. Hence, the commodity will be cheaper to consumers—at least after some time if production cannot be adjusted immediately—and all those who would like to buy the commodity can do so. Finally, if a combination of the two objectives is sought, say increased consumption of a certain commodity among certain consumers, a more efficient method would be selective (for example, income graduated) subsidies. As an example, if a government wants to encourage low-income families with many children to get more dwelling space, the system of selective subsidies should be designed so that subsidies vary with family income and family size as well as with the actual size of the housing unit.

The choice of policy instruments to reach given objectives is also influenced, of course, by the administrative costs of the various policy alternatives. This aspect carries little weight in the present situation, however, since price regulation and the extensive supervision it requires belong to a relatively labour-intensive and, hence, to an expensive category of policy measures (see, for example, the regulated housing markets).

2.5.3 Summary

Compared to a system of equilibrium prices, government price regulation or private pricing agreements, which give rise to a permanent state of excess demand on a market, have as we have seen the following implications:

(a) unsatisfied demand;

(b) inefficient allocation of supply to consumers;

(c) the emergence of a black market and, hence, of unwarranted price differentiation;

(d) high transaction costs on the legal as well as the black markets;

(e) lack of output adjustment to changes in demand;

(f) lack of information about the true size of demand and, hence, inefficient planning of production.

These negative effects can be avoided and the objectives behind price regulation can still be attained if equilibrium pricing is restored and combined with a system of subsidies or transfers.

2.6 Imperfect Competition

As we have pointed out earlier, the real-world deviations from the perfect market economy model concern not only assumptions about commodity properties and production techniques but also the behaviour assumptions behind the model. In the preceding section we described one example of the latter type of deviation in the form of market disequilibrium. As we presented it, however, such imperfections were essentially the result of government behaviour.

This section deals with an important example of behavioural imperfection in realistic versions of the uncontrolled market economy. We shall be concerned with deviations from the assumption of perfect competition, that is, from the assumption that the number of buyers and sellers on each market is sufficiently large to make it impossible for any single behaviour unit to influence market prices.

Imperfect competition may appear in many different forms. It may occur on the seller side or on the buyer side of the market; it may involve only a few units of equal size or fairly many, or it may involve more complex structures such as one big and several small units, etc. We refrain from going into the particular consequences of each of these varieties. Instead, we intend to bring out the effects of what is common to all these forms of imperfect competition, that is the deviation from a purely market-determined price, due to the fact that the price is influenced or even determined by the individual unit. For this purpose, it will be sufficient to deal with the case of *one* seller (and many buyers) in a market.

2.6.1   Allocative Effects of Monopoly Behaviour

As already mentioned, a monopoly which maximises profits (over a certain period of time) produces and sells a volume of output at which marginal costs and marginal revenue coincide. This means that the out-

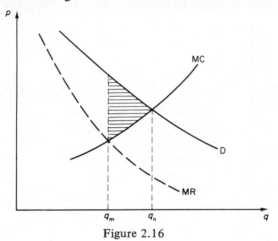

Figure 2.16

put will be less than optimal from the point of view of the economy as a whole. Allowing the area below the demand curve in figure 2.16 to express the consumers' maximum willingness to pay and the area under the marginal cost curve to represent social costs (opportunity costs) of production, we find that the difference between the two areas will show the *social surplus* of the commodity concerned (see the discussion in connection with figures 2.9 and 2.14). The shaded area in figure 2.16 will then express the social loss, which results because the monopoly does not extend its output to the point where price and marginal costs are equalised[†].

---

† It should be observed that monopoly firms are also subjected to some competition, namely competition from the potential entry of other producers as well as from producers of *other* goods. And the more intense the latter kind of competition is, the more sensitive to price changes is the demand for the monopolist's commodity, and the smaller the social loss of monopoly behaviour.

This loss, however, is not the only adverse effect of monopoly behaviour on resource allocation. In addition, high profits and other consequences of limited competition can be expected to give rise to a wasteful use of available resources and hence to an unnecessarily high level of production costs. The monopolist, in other words, may not regard feasible increases in profits as a sufficiently strong motive for 'unpopular' reorganisations within the company. In this perspective, and with the implicit assumption that reorganisation measures in themselves do not require large inputs of resources, the marginal costs in figure 2.16 turn out to be too high. In a hypothetical situation of active competition,

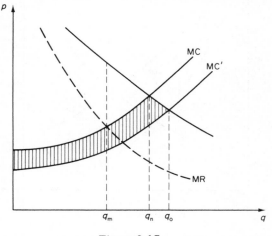

Figure 2.17

say on a larger market, the marginal costs might be reduced to the level indicated by the MC' curve in figure 2.17.

The monopoly would thus lead to a second form of efficiency loss as shown by the shaded area in figure 2.17 (reduced by the costs, if any, for reorganising production). This loss can be specified as follows. Reductions could be made in the costs of the original volume of output q_m as well as in the costs for increases up to the output q_n, optimal according to the presentation in figure 2.16. However, with a lower level of marginal costs, the optimal output must increase from q_n to q_o in order for the social surplus to be maximised. And this, in turn, means that the *total* efficiency loss from monopoly behaviour will equal the sum of the shaded areas in both figures 2.16 and 2.17.

Exercise.   Give a verbal explanation why the social surplus must increase with a change in output from q_n to q_o.

The empirical evidence of the size of the efficiency losses discussed is both fragmentary and open to criticism. It is often assumed, however, that the loss from limited competition is due primarily to the second effect, that is the reduced cost efficiency. Moreover, it is sometimes argued that the first effect—underproduction due to monopolistic pricing policy—is of no practical importance. The efficiency loss that stems from this effect, it is suggested, amounts to much less than one per cent of the value of total production (GNP) in the economy. It should be observed, however, that even small percentages of the GNP in this context may be important from a policy point of view. What we are discussing here are policy measures which would imply more or less *permanent* elimination of limitations upon competition (or of its adverse effects). If, as a result of a particular policy intervention, competition were increased to the effect of a gain of 0·5 per cent of the GNP per year during a period of, say, 15 years, the sum of the yearly figures would correspond to some 10 per cent of the GNP in the initial year, a considerable yield for a single act of policy intervention. But it should be noted that this is a comment on the technique of measurement of the social costs of imperfect competition, not an attempt to estimate the actual size of these costs[†].

---

† To show formally how imperfect competition impedes the attainment of Pareto optimality, we shall reformulate the analysis of figure 2.17. Let us now define demand for commodity 1 with respect to the price of the commodity in relation to the price of other commodities p_c, that is, with respect to the *relative* price p_1/p_c. As consumers are considered to be in equilibrium, regardless of the actual prices, a point on the demand curve thus implies that

$$MRS^i_{c1} = \frac{p_1}{p_c}$$

Similarly, costs of production for commodity 1 may be expressed relative to the amount of other commodities that has to be given up in order to produce more of commodity 1. MC′ in figure 2.17 thus represents the amount of other goods given up in order to produce an additional unit of output of the monopoly firm. This means that MC′ expresses the marginal rate of transformation between commodity 1 and other commodities. Now, as monopoly behaviour makes $p_1/p_c >$ MC′ (see the figure), the marginal rate of transformation must deviate from p_1/p_c and hence from the marginal rate of substitution. The condition for Pareto optimality—that marginal rates of transformation and of substitution should be equal—is therefore fulfilled only when prices equal marginal costs (see page 15 and appendix 1, page 137).

2.6.2   Policy measures

The question now arises as to whether there are practicable means of eliminating imperfect competition and hence, eliminating the social loss described in the previous section. In the particular case where the monopoly firm discussed above consists of a large number of similar plants capable of being operated as separate and independent firms, legislative action in the form of *anti-trust policy* would be sufficient. One disadvantage related to measures of this kind, however, is that they often tend to be slow and sometimes easy to circumvent.

If many individual companies can exist in the market, as we have assumed, an alternative (or complement) to legislative action would be to initiate the establishment of new and competing companies or to provide conditions favourable to the emergence of new competitors. Specifically, this may take the form of introducing government operated companies, of subsidising private or cooperative companies or of initiating structural changes on the credit market to facilitate the entry of new companies, for example, through the creation of special government banks. There is a widespread opinion, but little systematic evidence, that cost efficiency tends to be low in enterprises of this kind. (If this is true, the reason may be that the government is always there to provide more or less inexhaustible financial support). Therefore, it is possible that measures of this kind alone cannot eliminate the entire social loss of imperfect competition.

Now there is not always room for many individual companies on a market of the kind we are discussing here. A typical state is rather that one single company, due to economies of scale, has considerable advantages in terms of efficiency (see section 2.3). In these cases, the natural course may appear to be to nationalise the monopoly. But this solution, as well as the more sophisticated one of regulating a private monopoly by fiscal policy measures, has the disadvantage of being unable to guarantee a high level of cost efficiency.

Exercise.   Try to explain how unit subsidies in combination with taxes on profits can be used to guide a private monopoly towards a higher volume of output without increasing the net profits of the monopoly.

In some cases, however, it may be possible to arrange for many companies to compete for the *right* to be the sole producer on the market and to give a time-limited concession to the company with the lowest price bid. This solution would, under ideal circumstances at least, lead to a level of efficiency close to that obtained in a (hypothetical situation of perfect competition.

To sum up, there are various ways of increasing output from a less than optimal level in an industry with imperfect competition. But it is unlikely that such policies will bring forth the kind of cost efficiency described above.

2.6.3   Long-term Effects of 'Antitrust Policy'

As we have indicated, feasible policy measures to promote competition or to avoid the adverse effects of imperfect competition are far from perfect. Thus, in practice, the social gain from combating restrictions of competition falls short of its theoretical maximum. The strength of anti-trust policy turns out to be even more limited if the fact that policy measures may have adverse long-term effects as well is taken into account.

It can be argued that *restricted* competition creates conditions favourable to rapid growth of cost efficiency in the long term. The reason is that the alternative, strong competition, can be assumed to prevent the companies from taking actions other than those primarily aimed at survival in the short term. Entrepreneurs facing strong competition may simply lack time for long-term planning and for undertaking more elaborate projects of research and development. Moreover, in a situation of heavy competitive pressure, profits are usually so low that little room is left for the internal financing of research and development activities. Internal funds play a crucial role in this context as the possibilities of borrowing money for risky projects of this type are limited.

The fact that restricted competition can thus be seen to provide favourable conditions for measures promoting a more rapid technical change does not imply, however, that such measures will actually be taken. Without any incentives to undertake changes—which is something that restricted competition, as we mentioned above, cannot be expected to provide—there is no guarantee that the favourable conditions will have any effect.

We may now proceed to observe that barriers to the emergence of future monopoly positions may have harmful effects on incentives. According to established theories of economic development, it is the expectations of large profits in a future monopoly position that make companies experiment and introduce new goods and new methods of production. If the management of a company believes that large profits simply cannot be obtained in the future, it is likely to be more reluctant to undertake pioneering efforts, thus curtailing the growth rate of the company.

The efficiency problems of limited competition that we have dealt with so far are perhaps not the most significant ones. More important cases may be found in a regional context. If, in a certain area, only a limited number of employers is conceivable, thus implying limited competition for local labour, the individual firm will have a strong bargaining position against a government (local or national) that gives top priority to creating employment opportunities. This may easily develop into a situation where firms more or less count on subsidies or other favourable treatment from the government when they run into difficulties. If so, firms will be sheltered from the effects of outside competition and they will be kept alive even when they are incapable of using available resources efficiently. By contrast, large population centres with their differentiated economic activity make it possible for labour laid-off by one firm or industry to be absorbed by the expansion of other firms; hence, an efficient utilisation of resources is allowed for more or less continuously. And in these areas, firms cannot count on government support simply because they are able to provide job opportunities.

We may conclude by mentioning an important case of imperfect competition at another level. It concerns the giant international firms which tend to live their own lives outside the reach of any single national government. An individual country, particularly if it is small, hardly dares to intervene into the affairs of these multinational companies as such a policy might have far-reaching implications both in terms of employment opportunities and the inflow of foreign exchange.

2.6.4 Summary

Limited competition in an industry tends to keep output as well as production costs off optimal levels. Taken together, these two effects may give rise to a heavy loss of social efficiency. We have seen, however, that feasible countermeasures are imperfect or may have substantial adverse side-effects. Moreover, limited competition—or at least the prospects of such a situation in the future—may be favourable to technical change in the industry. This is not to say, however, that these aspects are important enough to disqualify anti-trust policy and similar forms of government intervention.

2.7 Imperfect Information

It is a much debated issue whether or not people in a market economy can be said to have a free choice as consumers. A closely related point of controversy is whether or not production in a market economy is guided by consumer preferences. These issues, to put it bluntly, cannot be answered by a simple yes or no. With respect to *existing* and well-known goods, for example food products consumed daily, it seems fair to say that the individual consumer makes his free choice and that he contributes to the continuation or cessation of production activities. On the other hand, when it comes to commodities or product qualities that the market economy does not provide, due to imperfections of the type we have been discussing so far (certain effects of restricted competition, decreasing cost situations, collective commodity properties or negative external effects), but which an efficient economy *should* produce, it cannot be said, of course, that consumers have a free choice. Nor can it be said that consumers in the pure market economy are in a position to influence production decisions in these cases.

The two issues just mentioned often seem to relate to an aspect other than that of existing or non-existing commodities in a market economy. This aspect has to do with the specific question of whether people are actually informed about the content of various consumption alternatives and whether available information is misleading or not. We shall try to analyse in some detail how incomplete as well as misleading information affects consumer choice. In addition, certain principles for a socially efficient volume and composition of consumer information will be discussed.

By observing that information may be imperfect, we make a further step towards reality and away from the assumptions of the perfect market economy model. Imperfect information will be seen to have many traits in common with the technical imperfections dealt with earlier. But in other respects, it has special characteristics, which make it appropriate to let imperfect information constitute a category of its own.

2.7.1   Effects of Imperfect Information on Consumer Choice

In this section, we study certain consequences of four different kinds of imperfect information: imperfect information about prices, about the existence of a commodity, about the properties ('quality') of a commodity and, finally, imperfect information due to so-called persuasive advertising. In all cases, the imperfections are assumed to refer to commodity 2, whereas the consumer is assumed to be completely informed with regard to the relevant aspects of commodity 1 ('other goods'). In order to simplify the analysis further, we shall assume that commodity 2 is purchased once, at the most. Moreover, in this section we disregard the individual consumer's costs for gathering and processing information.

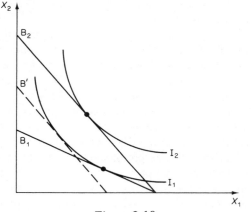

Figure 2.18

(a) Assume that the consumer *lacks information about the fact that commodity 2 is available at a lower price* from another nearby trader. In figure 2.18, B_1 represents the consumer's budget line at the known price and B_2 the budget line if he had known about the possibility of purchasing commodity 2 at the lower price. In the situation that actually prevails the consumer will be able to reach indifference curve I_1. If, on the other hand, he had obtained the additional information, he would have been able to reach I_2. The value of the missing information is therefore shown by the difference between I_2 and I_1. (For the time being, disregard the broken budget line B' in this and the subsequent figures.)

(b) Now, assume instead that the consumer *lacks information about the existence of commodity 2*. In that case, he will naturally consume commodity 1 only. In terms of figure 2.19 his indifference 'curves' and budget 'line' will appear as points along the X_1 axis. With point C indicating the amount of commodity 1 that his budget allows him to buy, he will be able to reach I_1. Had he known that commodity 2 existed, and had he known its properties, price, etc., he might have chosen to consume some of that commodity as well. Let us say that he would have chosen point D instead of point C. Thus, he would have reached a higher indifference curve, such as $I_2{'}$ if the true budget line were B_2. The consumer's loss due to imperfect information is therefore given by the difference between I_2 and I_1 (or $I_2{'}$ and $I_1{'}$).

(c) Assuming now that the consumer's *information about the properties of commodity 2* is imperfect, we obtain the situation illustrated

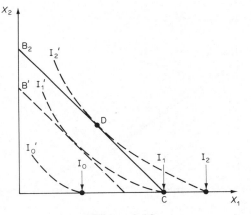

Figure 2.19

in figure 2.20. The indifference curves I_0, I_1, etc. refer to a case in which the consumer has exaggerated expectations with respect to the 'quality' of this commodity. Under these conditions, he chooses point E on his budget line. Later he will be disappointed and he will realise that his indifference curves, given perfect information to begin with, would have looked like $I_0{'}$, $I_1{'}$, etc. Thus, had he known beforehand what he knows now, he might have refrained from buying commodity 2 at all and chosen point F instead. The consumer's real loss due to lack of information in this case is shown by the difference between $I_1{'}$ and $I_0{'}$. (As seen from the point of view of his *expectations* at the time of the purchase (I_2), the loss would appear as the larger difference between I_2 and I_0. This estimate, however, is irrelevant as an expression of the gain to be obtained from correct information.)

(d) The situation just described can be used to illustrate the consequences of so-called *persuasive advertising*. Confronted with messages
of this kind, the consumer can be assumed to have obtained an overly
positive impression of commodity 2. This impression is assumed to be
rectified once he actually consumes the commodity. In terms of figure 2.2
he expected to reach I_2 but in fact only attained I_0'. Had it been possible
to neutralise the persuasive advertising he had been confronted with, he
could have reached I_1'. Thus, the real loss due to imperfect information
is once again equal to the difference between I_1' and I_0' in the figure.

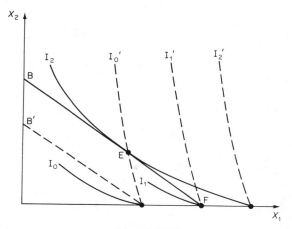

Figure 2.20

2.7.2   The Value of Additional Information

In the cases discussed in section 2.7.1, the value of the missing information was defined in abstract terms, that is, in terms of indifference curves.
This was a natural consequence of our purpose, which was to pin down
consumer behaviour in various situations of incomplete information.
This procedure becomes insufficient when we wish to establish the individual maximum willingness to pay for additional information. Estimates
in these terms are required to compare the value of information with
the costs of information and to discuss optimal individual and social
information levels.

    In principle, the maximum willingness to pay for additional pieces
of information of the kind discussed in the preceding section is given by
the income reduction, or downward shift of the budget line, that is large

enough to make it possible for the consumer with perfect information to reach the indifference curve actually attained without additional information. A shift of the budget line down to the broken line B' in figures 2.18, 2.19 and 2.20 represents this maximum amount in each case—that is, a shift from B_2 to B' in figure 2.18 and from B to B' in figures 2.19 and 2.20. These shifts have the same effects as reductions in consumer income and, hence, they can be expressed in terms of income or money.

Our initial assumption that commodity 2 is bought only once, if at all, is a necessary requirement (in cases (a) and (b) above) for the relevance of the information value as defined. Of course, if additional information had meant similar gains for repeated purchases in future periods, the maximum willingness to pay would have reached a correspondingly higher level.

Moreover, our calculation of the value of additional information was based on the more crucial assumption that it is practically feasible to know exactly what kind of information will be obtained by a specific act of information gathering on the part of the consumer. This, in fact, can only be determined in exceptional cases. One particular example is given by the case of consumer reports that are explicitly said to contain information about, say, two brands of vacuum cleaners of the same quality and yet differing in price by £10. When seeking reports of this kind, the consumer interested in buying a vacuum cleaner can be said to know what kind of information he gets and what it is worth to him.

In a hypothetical case in which the individual consumer always knows what he would get out of an additional effort to gather information at a known cost, it would be a simple matter to define his optimum information activity. Information should be accumulated as long as the cost of an additional effort to collect information falls short of this maximum willingness to pay for the additional information so collected. It would then also be possible to assume that the individual consumer could arrive at an optimum position without outside help.

Now the consumer normally cannot know the value of an additional effort to obtain information without, in fact, knowing the precise content of the resulting piece of information. But if he knew the content, he would not need to acquire the additional piece of information. Thus, information differs from other commodities in the sense that the consumer cannot have perfect information about the commodity and, at the same time, be willing to demand the commodity. Thus information as a demanded commodity presupposes (with the exception mentioned above) that the value of information is unknown. In fact, the consumer often has no idea whatsoever about (that is, cannot calculate an expected value from a known probability distribution for) the outcome of an attempt to obtain further information about, say, the price of a commodity at another source of supply—whether the price is higher or lower—or what he could actually gain by studying reports on commodity tests, etc. And, in cases such as these, economic theory fails to come up with an analysis of what might be considered optimal consumer behaviour As the returns on additional acts of information gathering are completely unknown, the optimum level of such acts cannot be determined with the help of conventional methods of optimisation; these methods require that it be possible, in principle at least, to specify the expected returns on additional consumer efforts to gain information. Hence, we shall have to regard individual information gathering under complete uncertainty as arbitrarily determined. Specifically, this means that information gathering will be determined on the basis of what is normally done ('look into 2 or 3 shops'), or what the consumer happens to do, or what he would do if he had 'arrived at' certain subjectively determined probabilities of different outcomes of additional efforts to obtain information[†].

2.7.3   Socially Efficient Information Activity

If the situation just described were also relevant to society as a whole, there would not be much more to say in terms of analysis. As it turns out, however, some important remarks on information activity from the point of view of social efficiency can be added.

(1) If individual consumers actually try to get information and if this activity requires a certain amount of resources, *centralised information gathering and information distribution* could be more efficient in the sense that the same amount of information could be obtained using less resources. This can be attained for example, when the same piece of information with respect to the properties of a certain commodity can serve a large number of consumers. In other words, these *economies of scale,* typical for information production, imply that decentralised infor-

---

[†] We have limited our discussion here to the information problem of the consumer. In principle, similar conclusions can be drawn with respect to producers, particularly as far as future commodity and factor prices are concerned. Producers' information about present market conditions seems to be less of a problem since companies normally may be assumed to have more resources for these purposes and more relevant technical know-how than individual consumers.

mation production is inefficient and that, given the amount of resources consumers want to devote to activities of this kind, an unnecessarily small information output would result from the process.

(2) Centralised information of the type just mentioned can sometimes be transferred to consumers in a private form, for example as printed reports from extensive tests of goods (such as automobiles) the properties of which are valued in different ways by different consumers. In other cases, information may be such that it cannot be effectively sold in a private form. This may apply, for example, to information about the least expensive source of supply of a certain commodity. If one consumer has received this piece of information, he may be expected to pass it on to others without charge. In other words, consumers other than those actually paying for a particular piece of information will benefit from it in this case. Thus, information of this kind emerges as a public good (cf. the definition on page 32) which, as we have seen, the market economy cannot be expected to provide to an efficient extent, if at all. In contrast to the case dealt with under point (1), this kind of information activity has to be financed by the public sector.

(3) In certain cases of persuasive advertising the individual consumers cannot be expected to be capable of neutralising the content of the messages received. It may then be in the interest of consumers that legislative actions be taken, for example, regulations against 'deceptive' marketing practices or laws requiring sellers to provide standardised descriptions of commodity properties or informative labelling. The government may find, however, that it does not want to try to abolish or reduce this kind of advertising after all. This may be because of anticipated negative side-effects such as a delay in the introduction of new commodities. In such cases, social efficiency may be promoted if the government intervenes instead on the recipients' side of the information 'market', for example, by training consumers to resist persuasive advertising[†].

(4) So far we have discussed government intervention in the information process concerning commodities as they would appear in an unregulated market economy. Now, it may be compatible with social

---

† The ability to neutralise persuasive advertising as well as the overall ability to gather and analyse information may be less developed among certain consumer groups, low-income earners in particular. It may, therefore, be considered as a distributional objective to take actions making information easier to digest (for example, by compulsory and standardised commodity labelling) and/or to train (future) consumer in schools or otherwise.

efficiency to reduce product differentiation—and, hence limit the number of commodities marketed—by introducing *standards* with which commodities must comply. This would tend to lessen the need for information. A reduction of product differentiation may be carried out without diminishing competition among producers; in fact, competition would be stimulated by the introduction of such standards insofar as this would bar producers from creating 'watertight' monopolistic submarkets for their specific product varieties.

Information activity implies, as we have pointed out, that resources are used for gathering, compiling, processing and transferring data. The mere existence of such real costs makes it unlikely that *complete* information will be efficient from the consumers' point of view, that is that it will be socially efficient. In fact, it is not more likely than that complete satiation of an ordinary commodity is socially efficient. Moreover, we must observe here that information activities are time-consuming and that the consumers' time budget is limited. So, even if information about all consumption alternatives (including data on prices, quality, etc.) did not involve any costs of the kind mentioned above the individual consumer could not be expected to have enough time or to want to spend the time necessary for acquiring complete information.

Thus, even taking aspects of social efficiency into account, we find that optimal information is incomplete information. This conclusion must now be confronted with our assumption on page 1 of a 'sufficient' degree of consumer information. This assumption was intended to mean that information about prices and commodity properties could be regarded as complete for those commodities that could be expected to interest the individual consumer. The assumption was used to show, among other things, that an equilibrium position in a perfect market economy is characterised by a Pareto-optimal allocation. If, now, information is imperfect, prices for homogeneous goods will not necessarily be uniform, since imperfect information allows high-price firms to remain on the market; hence, an equality among producers' marginal rates of transformation will not arise. Moreover, imperfect information may impede equality between true marginal rates of substitution for two commodities and the corresponding price relation (as shown in figure 2.20).

Thus, we see that the model of the perfect market economy is incapable of providing an exact picture of reality in these respects also. The fact still remains, however, that this model is a useful approximation of feasible states in large parts of the real-world economy and that it provides a simple starting-point for analysing imperfections in the real world. One example of this is the way we have tried to use the model in this chapter.

2.7.4 Summary

The lack of information about the existence of commodities and their prices and properties can be said to force the consumer to a lower in-difference curve than would be possible with perfect information. Since information as a commodity differs from other demanded commodities in that perfect information about information is an inadmissible assumption, the efficiency problem cannot be analysed using the same simple methods we have applied so far. Given, however, that information requires inputs of resources and time, we may assert that complete information is incompatble with social efficiency. Furthermore, if incomplete information is said to imply that consumers do not have a completely free choice, we may also assert that a completely free choice is not in the interest of the consumers.

The unregulated market economy cannot be expected to generate information in an efficient way. Economies of scale for information production call for centralisation, which in turn calls for public control in order to avoid monopoly pricing. Moreover, the fact that certain kinds of information appear as public goods implies that information production has to be financed by the government in order to be efficiently organised or in order to exist at all.

Economic-policy measures that can alter the information activity of the market economy consist of public information production, subsidisation of centralised commodity tests and commodity information, legislative actions against deceptive marketing practices, compulsory commodity labelling, standardisation of commodities and training of consumers.

2.8 The 'Imperfect' Economy

In this chapter we have discussed various deviations from the technical and behavioural postulates of the perfect market economy model as well as from its assumptions about information. We have shown that the effects of these deviations make it impossible for the *laissez-faire* market economy to attain a state of social efficiency. However, as we have also shown, economic policy (allocation policy) can be applied to help the economy reach an efficient state. At the same time, we have realized that putting these possibilities of intervening into the functioning of the market economy into effect is not always favourable. This became clear in particular when we discussed various methods for avoiding the effects of market imperfections due to limited competition. To sum up our arguments on this point, we have suggested that there are at least two factors that tend to reduce the desirability of allocation policy measures of the type discussed in this chapter.

(1) Policy measures give rise to real costs for information, control and administration in general. These 'policy costs' may reach a level at which they outweigh the ensuring policy benefits.

(2) Policy intervention may reduce the rates of innovation and technical improvements in general. The benefits of an efficient use of resources today may thus be outweighed by adverse effects in the long term. Or, as it is sometimes put, *static* efficiency or short-term efficiency (which we have called efficiency, pure and simple) may be inconsistent *dynamic* or long-term efficiency, that is a high rate of technical change[†].

Thus, in both cases (1) and (2) there are factors that may balance or outweigh the gains in terms of efficiency from allocation policy. Similar problems of counteracting effects will be encountered in chapter 3, where certain measures desirable in the context of stabilisation and distribution policy are shown to have negative effects on efficiency (see in particular section 3.1.4).

Before entering into these problems, it should be stressed that it was in an attempt to keep the discussion in the present chapter uncompli- cated that we have analysed each imperfection against the background of an 'otherwise perfect economy'. When there is some, for political reasons incorrigible, imperfection elsewhere in the economy (for example, in any of the six respects mentioned in this chapter or due to an economic policy that prevents efficiency) our conclusions have to be modified. It then becomes a question of attempting in each separate case to arrive at a

---

† We have seen that this aspect becomes highly important when considering a more active antitrust policy. But it is significant in other contexts as well. Two examples: (a) Prohibiting commercial advertising in order to reduce misleading consumer information and thus allow for social efficiency, would, at the same time, reduce the possibilities for new commodities to be introduced and hence may be detrimental to consumer interests. (b) Eliminating patent laws would improve the spread of innovations, but it would also reduce the expected profits from research and development projects and hence reduce the willingness to undertake such projects.

'second-best' position for the economy. However, this in no way implies that the criteria mentioned in this chapter always become obsolete or that their characteristics change. In general, it is 'simply' a matter of modifying the analysis so that costs and benefits are based on specially estimated prices ('shadow prices') instead of on the basis of the directly observable market prices, which under these circumstances are no longer an expression for social marginal costs (marginal resource use) or consumers' valuation of marginal changes. (See chapter 4 for examples of this approach.)

3. EFFICIENCY ASPECTS OF EMPLOYMENT AND DISTRIBUTION POLICY

Our discussion so far may be summarised as follows. An economy, which is capable of adjusting quickly to equilibrium positions and in which the actual income distribution is the desired one, does not need any economic policy other than the allocation policy discussed in chapter 2, that is, policy measures aimed at making the allocation Pareto optimal in equilibrium positions. In reality, however, adjustments to equilibrium positions are often quite slow; chronic unemployment, general or local, is perhaps the most significant example here. Moreover, the actual distribution of real income is often considered to be far off the target. Hence, the government intervenes, in practice, to stabilise employment, etc., as well as to redistribute income. The purpose of this chapter is to analyse efficiency aspects of this kind of government intervention.

In section 3.1 we shall show how acts of distribution policy and stabilisation policy may impede social efficiency. Specifically, we demonstrate how various kinds of taxes make it impossible to fulfil the conditions for Pareto optimality mentioned earlier. In section 3.2 we discuss some specific areas of distribution policy and show how policy instruments may differ in adequacy—or efficiency—with respect to the attainment of given distribution goals.

3.1 Allocative Effects of Tax Policy

There are at least four reasons for the existence of taxes:

(1) *Stabilisation*—taxes are introduced and changed in order to attain and maintain a position of high employment, price stability and balance between exports and imports;

(2) *Distribution*—taxes, including, for example, a system of progressive income taxes can be used to achieve a desired relative income redistribution;

(3) *Merit wants*—the government may hold the view that the individual consumer, in certain respects, does not know what is good for him and may use taxes to make him reduce his consumption of certain 'harmful' commodities such as tobacco or alcohol (see page 131);

(4) *Allocation*—production that creates negative effects on, say, the natural environment may be subjected to specific taxes in order to achieve efficiency; in this way, market prices are modified to reflect the real social costs of production[†].

Starting with motive (4) it is obviously true that taxes in this sense are designed to improve the allocation of resources, that is to meet the conditions for Pareto optimality. With respect to taxes based on the existence of merit wants (motive 3), it can be said that they improve or distort the allocation of resources depending on whether this intervention into consumer preferences is accepted or rejected. As far as the first two motives are concerned, it is our purpose in this section to demonstrate that taxes of this kind tend to distort resource allocation, that is, to impede fulfilment of the Pareto conditions. First of all we look into the effects of an excise tax (a tax on a particular commodity) introduced for, say, stabilisation purposes. In a second step, we deal with the allocative effects of income taxes.

3.1.1   Allocative Effects of Excise Taxes

The nature of allocative distortions that arise from the introduction of excise taxes is well illustrated by the following example (taken from Paul A. Samuelson's *Economics*). Centuries ago, residential property taxes were based on the number of windows in the house. The objective was to let the tax vary with the size of the house, given that large houses had many windows. The natural consequence of this tax system was that houses came to be built with a minimum of windows—which in turn caused the government to increase the tax rate per window. Obviously

---

† It may surprise some readers that this list does not contain the financial motive that 'taxes are required for government expenditure'. This exclusion is consciously made, however. Contrary to popular belief, a strict relationship of this kind does not exist; government expenditure need not be financed by taxes. Simply stated, it can be said that aspects of stabilisation determine how much of the expenditure (perhaps even more than 100 per cent) should be covered by taxes, or better, the extent to which the purchasing power elsewhere in the economy has to be reduced by taxes in particular, in order to make resources available for satisfying the wants of the public sector while maintaining a stable economy.

it would have been better in this case if the same amount of property taxes had been raised without 'forcing' people to live in darkness.

We now show formally how an excise tax makes it impossible to attain a Pareto optimum. If a tax amounting to $£tp_1$ per unit of commodity 1 is introduced, the consumer price, p_1, and the producer (net) price, $p_1(1 - t)$, will differ. If the rest of the economy is perfect, consumers will adjust their behaviour so that their marginal rates of substitution will be equal to the new price ratios. Taking commodities 1 and 2 as examples, we obtain

$$MRS^i_{21} = \frac{p_1}{p_2}$$

Producers make a similar adjustment to the price ratio relevant to them, that is

$$MRT^j_{21} = \frac{p_1(1 - t)}{p_2}$$

This means that $MRS^i_{21} \neq MRT^j_{21}$ and hence, that the conditions for Pareto optimality will not be fulfilled (see chapter 1).

This result, the distorting effect of an excise tax, is illustrated in figure 3.1. For simplicity, it is assumed here that there are only one consumer and one producer, although they are taken to behave as if

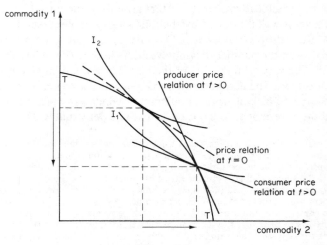

Figure 3.1

there were many of each. The TT-curve in the figure indicates as usual the set of efficient production possibilities for the two commodities, while I_2 shows the highest indifference curve attainable when consumer and producer prices coincide. Conversely, when consumer and producer prices differ by a tax (on commodity 1 in our case), this optimum point cannot be reached. This can be explained as follows. Diagrammatically speaking, the value of t determines the deviation in slope between the consumer's and the producer's price lines. Both lines, the slopes of which are thus held in a constant relationship, must now be shifted from the initial point (relevant for $t = 0$) to the new equilibrium point where producer profits are maximised and, simultaneously, the consumer reaches his highest feasible indifference curve (I_1). Hence, due to the introduction of the tax, the consumer will be forced down from I_2 to I_1, thereby changing his consumption pattern to one with more of commodity 2 and less of the taxed commodity 1.

Exercise. Demonstrate why the distortive effect of a given tax is smaller where price elasticities of supply and demand are low, that is, where supply and demand curves are steep[†]. Show also in which two special cases the introduction of an excise tax has no distortive effects.

3.1.2 Allocative Effects of Income Taxes

We could show that by introducing a temporary tax on all consumer goods, a kind of sales tax, we would get a distortive effect similar to that discussed in the preceding section, but this time against consumption in general and in favour of saving. (It should be noted that this 'distortion' may be desirable in another perspective, for example, in the context of stabilisation policy.)

Now, if saving were primarily intended for future consumption and if the sales tax were expected to remain in the future, we may disregard the distortive effect just mentioned, since the shift from consumption to saving no longer would mean that sales taxes were evaded, only postponed. Instead, we may note that a tax system of this kind closely resembles an income tax system, saving and consumption being taxed to (approximately) the same extent. Although we confine ourselves to a

---

† Note that low elasticities in this context reflect the difficulty of shifting production from one commodity to another and of substituting consumption of one commodity for consumption of another, respectively. Thus, the elasticities reflect the shape of the transformation and indifference curves, respectively.

discussion of the distortive effects of income taxes, we are thus also able
to shed some light on the distortive effects of sales taxes as they often
tend to appear in the real world.

An individual who acts as if he were trying to reach the highest indifference curve possible and who, at least approximately, is in a position
to adjust his working time (including moonlighting) will increase his
working time up to the point where his marginal rate of substitution between leisure time (F) and, say, commodity 1 equals the price ratio between the two. In this case, the price ratio is given by the 'price of
leisure time', equal to ratio of the wage rate after taxes, $p_w(1 - t_w)$, and
the price of commodity 1 (see chapter 1). Hence

$$MRS^i_{1F} = \frac{p_w(1 - t_w)}{p_1}$$

As usual, companies are assumed to hire labour up to the point at which
the value of the marginal product of labour inputs equals the wage rate
(before income taxes), that is up to the point where

$$MRT^j_{1F} = MP^j_{1F} = \frac{p_w}{p_1}$$

Hence, the condition for Pareto optimality $MRS^i_{1F} = MRT^j_{1F}$, *cannot be
fulfilled in the presence of an income tax,* that is with $t_w > 0$.

An income tax can thus be said to imply a 'tax on work'. We now
investigate whether this means that the volume of work will be reduced
by such a tax. If so, this would be compatible with the consequences of
the taxes discussed above whereby the taxpayer was seen to reduce his
consumption or holdings, etc., of the object of taxation. Such an outcome would also be in agreement with the familiar statement that 'it
does not pay to work' when income taxes are increased.

In order to give a simple answer to the question about the effects of
(increased) income taxes on the working time of the individual, we deal
with the case of an *introduction of a proportional income tax.*

Prior to the introduction of this tax, the individual may choose any
combination of leisure time and consumer goods shown by the BB' curve
in figure 3.2 (compare figure 1.4, section 1.2 for an explanation of this
diagram). This budget line may be explained by departing from point B.
In choosing this point, the individual would spend all his time on leisure
and, consequently, he would not earn any wages to spend on consumer
goods. By reducing leisure time from what it amounts to at point B, that
is by beginning to work, he will earn an income to spend on consumer

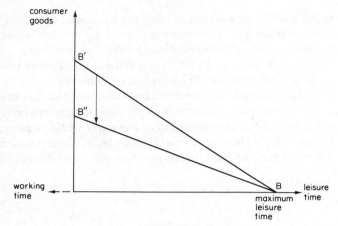

Figure 3.2

goods; the slope of the BB' curve that he then starts climbing is deter-mined by his wage rate.

Assume now that a proportional income tax is introduced with a tax rate of t_w. This results in a downward twist of the budget line to B''. The BB'' curve thus portrays income after taxes at different levels of working time. If point A shows the combination of work and leisure chosen at $t_w = 0$, that is prior to the introduction of the tax, we may now distin-guish between two alternative outcomes, as shown in figures 3.3 and 3.4.

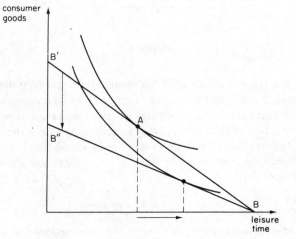

Figure 3.3

In figure 3.3 working time is reduced after the tax is introduced whereas the opposite outcome can be observed in figure 3.4. On closer inspection, it can be seen that the different outcomes are due to the different shapes of the indifference curves in the two cases, that is, to differences in individual preferences with respect to leisure and consumption.

We may thus conclude that the desired working time may decrease or increase when an income tax is introduced or when income tax rates are increased. A more intuitive explanation of this result would run along the following lines. An income tax makes work less remunerative, which in itself tends to favour leisure: the substitution effect. At the same time,

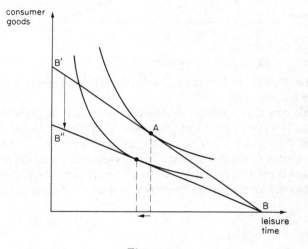

Figure 3.4

however, the tax will reduce after-tax income for a given amount of working time, which decreases the consumption of all commodities with a positive income elasticity, hence also leisure: the income effect.† If the income effect of the tax (implying a decrease in leisure time) exceeds the substitution effect (implying an increase in leisure time), the net effect will be a decrease in leisure time, that is, an increase in working time, and vice-versa.

† Income elasticity = $\dfrac{\text{change in demand (in percent)}}{\text{income change (in percent)}}$

Thus, a positive income elasticity for a commodity simply implies that demand increases when income is increased.

As we have pointed out, the net effect of an income tax on the desired level of working time depends on the shape of consumer preferences. Whether a change in actual working time will materialise depends largely on the individual's practical possibilities of making (small) adjustments in his working time. In reality, of course, these possibilities are quite limited for most employees. It should be observed, however, that effects of the kind we have discussed here may take the form of an adjustment of the volume of extra work or of a transition from (to) half-time to (from) full-time employment or of entering or leaving the labour market. These forms of discrete changes are conceivable for most people in the labour force.

3.1.3   Are There Neutral Taxes?

As we have seen, all of the tax systems discussed so far have distortive effects on resource allocation. This means that a government using this kind of policy instrument actually introduces an imperfection into the economy similar to the imperfections studied in chapter 2, which there called for neutralising government intervention. We may therefore raise the question of whether there are, in fact, taxes which are neutral with respect to resource allocation, that is, do not violate the conditions for Pareto optimality.

In passing, we may note that we have already touched upon two exceptional cases of (quasi) neutral taxes. Excise taxes at low price elasticities of supply or demand and income taxes in the presence of institutional barriers to adjustments of individual working time would, as we have seen, avoid (noticeable) distortions of resource allocation. But the only tax that would invariably be neutral with respect to the allocation of resources is a so-called lump-sum tax. In this case, individual tax amounts are given and thus not related to any part of individual economic activity. As an example, all individuals are called upon to pay an equal amount of tax. The practical use of a tax system of this kind is obviously very limited; the goals of economic policy in general, and of distribution policy in particular, imply that tax amounts should differ among individuals and, moreover, that they should differ in a systematic way, for example be related to the size of individual income or wealth.

Our conclusion is therefore that, given the presence of a policy of income and/or wealth redistribution among taxpayers, an altogether neutral tax system does not exist. Against this background, the objective of efficient taxation is to select taxes that reduce the distortive effects of allocation to a minimum.

3.1.4   Summary

We have seen that, except for a few cases of very limited scope, the kinds
of taxes that are used in practice to pursue a policy of stabilisation and
redistribution violate the Pareto optimum conditions and hence impede
an efficient allocation of resources. This is another example of the fact
that not only individual firms and consumers but also 'the supervisors
of the market economy', national and local governments, create imperfections in the functioning of the economy (see the discussion of government price regulations in section 2.5). One implication of this fact is
that a political decision must be made as to whether attaining a par-

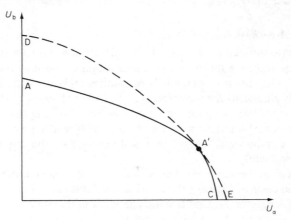

Figure 3.5

ticular stablisation or distribution policy goal is worth more than the
sacrifices required in terms of efficiency.

The main conclusions of our discussion in this section can be summarised by means of figure 3.5. In this figure, Pareto optimal points
are represented by the broken line DE. As in figure 1.3, U_a and U_b stand
for ordinal indices, that is, indices that express individual rankings of
feasible alternatives. To keep the exposition simple we assume a population of two persons only, a and b. In using a particular tax system, we
are in reality unable to advance further out than is indicated by the AC
curve in the attempt to reach a Pareto optimum. A$'$ represents the initial
position of a perfect market economy as well as the exceptional case in
which no measures of distribution or of stabilisation policy are taken.

In those cases in which there are several alternative policy approaches
to a specific policy goal, the problem amounts to finding that system of

taxes (or other policy instruments) which has a minimum of detrimental effects on resource allocation, that is which allows the highest possible level of social efficiency.

In the next section, we turn to a study of some concrete cases of distribution policy in order to provide more detailed insight into the problem of choosing the most efficient policy alternative.

3.2   Efficiency Aspects of Distribution Policy

To some people, it may appear irrelevant to demand maximum efficiency when the objective is to achieve a 'just' distribution of income or wealth in society. On closer inspection, this is a doubtful argument, perhaps most readily seen once we observe that in general the higher the level of efficiency the more there will be to transfer to those it is desired to favour, given the amount that is to be taken away from others.

In this section we shall analyse specific areas of distribution policy from an efficiency point of view. In each case we want to find out whether one particular policy instrument is more efficient than another in reaching a given objective of distribution policy. Our examples are taken from four different areas of distribution policy. They concern, in turn, income distribution within a region, among regions, among generations and among nations. Firstly, we shall discuss two alternative ways of supporting low-income families, conventional welfare policy and a system of so-called negative income taxes (including a guaranteed minimum income). Secondly, we shall deal with interregional distribution issues by comparing two alternative forms of regional policy. Thirdly, intergenerational income distribution policy is discussed from the point of view of measures aimed at increasing the total volume of real investments in the economy. Finally, we shall observe aspects of international income distribution by attempting to analyse efficiency aspects of government aid to poor countries.

It should be pointed out that the following four sections differ from other parts of this book in that the exposition is often rather argumentative. This is a natural consequence of the fact that we are now trying to deal with specific and concrete problems rather than with basic principles in general terms.

3.2.1   Are Negative Taxes an Efficient Form of Welfare Policy?

A central problem for welfare policy concerns the choice between aid in money and aid in kind. We start by commenting on this more general issue.

In figure 3.6, an attempt is made to illustrate the situation for an individual whom the government would like to help. Let us assume there are only two commodities. Commodity 1 can be thought of as food and commodity 2 as alcoholic beverages. If the individual is given an amount $\bar{x}_1$ of commodity 1, say, in the form of food stamps and if his own income thus allows him to buy $\bar{x}_2$ of commodity 2 he will reach point P.

Now, we assume that with the given conditions of production the economy can substitute commodity 1 for commodity 2 according to the line RS. In other words, the slope of this curve indicates the social marginal rate of transformation (MRT_{21}). When market prices coincide

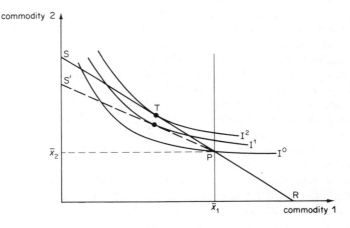

Figure 3.6

with the marginal rate of transformation and when the individual is given the same amount of support as before but this time in cash, he will be able to reach point T on the budget line RS. (The points P and T imply the same amount of support in the sense that in both cases society reverves the same amount of resources to meet the demand from the person being supported.) He thus reaches indifference curve I^2 instead of I^0, as in the preceding case. This means that the individual clearly prefers assistance in cash to an equally costly support in kind.

This conclusion holds even if the support in kind (the food stamps) can be sold on the 'black market'. Normally, the price offered will be unfavourable to the seller, as indicated by the budget line RPS'. He is now able to reach a point superior to the initial position, say on I^1

instead of I^0 in the diagram. But, as we can see, the improvement will not be as large as when assistance is given in cash.

To arrive at these conclusions, we have assumed that the government accepts the preferences of the welfare recipients. But, as we have pointed out earlier, the government may want to guide individual consumption patterns. For example, the government might want to reduce the consumption of commodity 2 (alcoholic beverages), thereby disqualifying the consumer's preference for point T. Thus, once the valuations of the donor and the recipient differ, support in kind may turn out to be superior to support in cash. In the rest of this section, however, we maintain our assumption that the welfare recipients' preferences are accepted by the government.

In most industrial countries, welfare policy means that relief is given —in cash or in kind—to persons who have themselves contacted the authorities and who have been able to demonstrate a specific kind of need accepted as valid ground for government support. Normally, these 'acceptable' forms of need refer to certain kinds of unemployment, illness, absence of a family head, etc. Traditional welfare policy thus implies a screening of applicants so that people with certain kinds of need are 'rewarded' while others are not.

If the value premises on which distribution policy is based imply that only people with specific kinds of need should be eligible for support, traditional policy measures may appear to be efficient in at least one respect: those who are not eligible for support are not given any help (aside from pure cases of fraud). On the other hand, the traditional welfare system may have been *in*efficient in two other respects.

Firstly, it seems to be evident by now that far from all those who are eligible for support receive assistance within the framework of existing welfare programmes. To avoid an outcome of this kind, everyone concerned should be informed about his rights to government support. Furthermore, it would be necessary to fight moral inhibitions or social obstacles which tend to keep people from exercising their rights in this respect. According to empirical studies (for example, in Sweden) traditional welfare policy has failed in these respects and considerable numbers of people eligible for support have remained out of the reach of existing welfare programmes.

Secondly, criteria for assistance have been so crude that small changes in work income have sometimes led to larger changes in welfare payments in the opposite direction. In extreme but not unusual cases, welfare payments will cease completely when work income exceeds a certain level, while the whole amount of assistance is given below this level. Households whose incomes have been below this critical level for a certain period of time have thus been totally unrewarded for trying to increase their work incomes. It is also possible—as is often suggested by the critics of social welfare systems—that many households in this situation have realised what the consequences of their efforts to increase their incomes would be and have simply refrained from making such efforts. This behaviour induced by the system clearly deviates from what must be assumed to be the real intentions of the system, namely to help people temporarily so that they can help themselves in the long run.

It is quite possible, however, that in many instances the objectives of welfare policy have been such that inefficiency has appeared in another respect as well. If the purpose has been to support everyone who has a low income, *regardless* of the reason for this predicament (excluding special groups such as school children, servicemen, etc.) the traditional form of welfare policy has failed—that is to say, *regardless* of whether the reason is to be found among easily ascertained states such as lack of employment opportunities or states more difficult to define such as lack of psychic balance, unsatisfactory work conditions (from the individual person's point of view), etc. Persons whose poverty originates in factors belonging to the latter category are not formally eligible for assistance; in other words, low income has not constituted a *sufficient* condition for assistance. Or, it may be such that the definition of need and poverty has changed over time and that now, given the past increase in average living standards and hence a larger capacity for 'generosity', the concepts of need and poverty have been extended to include anyone with a low income.

Against this background, we may formulate the following four subtargets for welfare policy:

(1) to support those who are eligible for support;
(2) to avoid giving relief to those not eligible for support;
(3) to maintain individual incentives for earning a living, that is to maintain work incentives;
(4) to keep administrative costs for welfare policy at a low level.

All these subtargets are related to efficiency and are, in principle, completely separable from political values for determining which groups to support and with how much. What we would like to know in this perspective is whether an alternative to traditional welfare policy, a system of so-called negative income taxes, would meet a given distribution goal more efficiently.

A negative income tax means that an income earner (with possible exceptions) will receive payments if his income falls short of a certain level. His disposable income may then develop as shown in figure 3.7. Without any income earnings at all he will receive a maximum amount— a guaranteed minimum income—of, say, £1000 per year. If he earns an income of £1000, he will receive an amount of, say £500, and so on up to a break-even level of income earned of, say £2000 at which no payments (negative taxes) are received, nor are any ordinary positive taxes paid. (The marginal negative income tax rate here is 50 per cent.) Above the before-tax income level of £2000 taxes are paid as usual[†].

Let us now investigate the extent to which the efficiency targets (1) to (4) can be achieved by a system of negative taxes as compared to a welfare policy of the traditional kind.

(1) As a system of negative income taxes implies that 'welfare payments' are tied to earnings, these payments can be arranged to be made more or less automatically, for example by a system of 'preliminary payments', a kind of negative withholding tax. By contrast, as we have pointed out, traditional policy requires information and initiative on the part of the poor. Moreover, the means tests of traditional policy might be regarded as a humiliating process and might thus deter those who are entitled to support from actually trying to get it. This implies that the traditional welfare system will actually reach a smaller proportion of the

---

† Observe that the concept of (guaranteed) minimum income differs from the concept of minimum wage rates. The latter kind of regulation obviously affects only those who are employed. The minimum income guarantee, on the other hand, concerns everybody and thus also those who are unemployed; in fact, the term minimum income refers directly to the income level of the unemployed. It should be pointed out that minimum wage regulation has been used as an instrument of welfare policy in some countries for the purpose of supporting low-wage earners. However, one drawback of this system is that it creates unemployment owing to the fact that the equilibrium wage rate is exceeded (see note 1, page 42). Hence, some wage-earners—those who are still employed—will have their incomes increased, whereas others are fired because they are too expensive in relation to their productivity. This latter group whose earnings drop to zero is thus left at the mercy of other welfare policy arrangements that might exist.

A feasible—and perhaps far superior—alternative to minimum wage regulation would be to support incomes by transfer payments (for example within a system of negative taxes) and to support employment opportunities by flexible wages—or at least by the absence of minimum wage regulation—in order to reach a state of equilibrium or 'full employment'.

target population than a system of negative taxes and hence be less efficient in this respect.

(2) The risk of making welfare payments to those who are *not* eligible for support exists in a system of negative taxes in the sense that fraudulent income tax returns can now also be made by those who have very small earnings. This system, then, may turn out to be less efficient as far as unwanted welfare payments are concerned, even though there are also possibilities of fraud in the traditional welfare system.

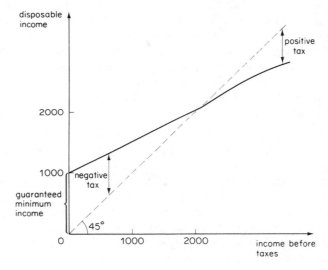

Figure 3.7

(3) It is sometimes suggested that incentives to work will be lower, or even disappear in some cases, under a system of negative taxes. Whether or not this is reasonable to assume would to some extent depend on the level of negative taxes. But even if quite substantial amounts were involved, full-time work could still be relied upon to provide a significantly higher level of disposable income, thus maintaining at least some work incentives. Furthermore, it must be observed that work is not only a way to make a living but also an opportunity to do something. For this reason alone we may expect voluntary unemployment to be kept at a low level. In fact, it seems quite possible to design a system of negative taxes so that work incentives would not be lower than in the traditional system. In the example we used in connection with figure 3.7, low-

income earners always retained 50 per cent of their earnings. Thus, the frustrating situation of a complete withdrawal of welfare payments in the presence of small changes in earnings, which we saw could happen under traditional welfare policy, need not arise here.

(4) The introduction of a system of negative income taxes would allow a reduction in the level of administrative costs. The traditional system with its complicated and labour-intensive 'means tests' would be replaced by a system of simple criteria. It should be observed, however, that negative taxes can by no means be said to meet all the requirements of a complete welfare system. For instance, it cannot meet the need for special measures with respect to particular groups of underprivileged people, such as the physically handicapped. The savings in administrative costs arising from the introduction of a negative income tax system can therefore be said to mean that more resources will be available for these specific fields of welfare policy.

A comparison between a system of negative taxes and those parts of traditional welfare policy that it would replace might be summarised as follows. Although the effects on work incentives are uncertain and although it is possible that more people will be given monetary support than actually intended, a system of negative income taxes would be more efficient in providing the target groups of poor people with economic assistance and in keeping administrative costs of welfare policy at a low level.

3.2.2   Subsidised Investments and Efficiency in Regional Economic Policy

Many countries have policies to create employment opportunities in depressed areas. For this end, governments often offer subsidies on new investments and/or provide favourable borrowing conditions to entrepreneurs willing to locate or to expand their business activities in such areas. Measures of this kind mean, first of all that it is the inputs of capital that are subsidised in these companies. Furthermore, subsidies are given only to companies that would otherwise close down or locate their activities in another area. In other words, profitable companies that already operate in the depressed areas do not have much chance of obtaining subsidies for an expansion of employment especially if this would take place within existing plants. We shall deal briefly with each of these two properties of regional policy.

It is obvious that regional policy runs the risk of being inefficient if all the alternatives for creating employment are not allowed to compete for government grants. In certain cases, it may definitely be less expensive for society (that is, smaller sacrifices in terms of net social output—and hence smaller subsidies or income transfer from taxpayers—are required per additional employment opportunity) to stimulate labour inputs in already profitable companies than to rely solely on companies that cannot survive without government support. From an efficiency point of view it is of little interest if the least expensive method for society—in the sense just mentioned—implies that profits increase in an already profitable company. Moreover, distribution policy is usually not concerned with supporting owners of 'poor' companies and withholding support from 'rich' companies.

Shifting to our second aspect of regional policy, the use of capital should not be subsidised if, as is the case here, the purpose is to stimulate labour utilisation at minimum costs in terms of net social output foregone per employment opportunity. This proposition may be illustrated by the following example.

Assume for simplicity that there is only one company in a certain region conceivable as a candidate for government support. We denote the labour input of this firm by L, the capital input by K and the level of output by q. The relationship between inputs and output, that is, the production function, can be written as

$$q = f(K, L)$$

(This means that the output q in a given, but here unspecified, way depends on the capital input K and the labour input L.) The output price is p, the wage rate is p_L and the cost of capital use is equal to r. Thus, the firm's profit equals

$$pf(K, L) - p_L L - rK$$

Let us also assume that the weights p, p_L and r are relevant in a social perspective as well; that is to say, they reflect the opportunity costs of the commodity produced and of the two inputs, respectively (see section 4.2). The policy target may then be formulated, 'maximise profits (or minimise losses), given that the available labour force in the region, $\bar{L}$, is employed by the firm.'

Now, as L should equal $\bar{L}$, the profit of the firm will depend solely on the level of capital inputs. In other words, maximum profit (minimum loss) will be attained by adjusting the K variable. And, as is well known from standard theory of the firm, maximum profit requires that capital inputs be increased up to the point where the value of the marginal product of capital (MP_K) equals the cost of capital use, that is to the point where

$$pMP_K = p\,\frac{\partial q}{\partial K} = r \qquad \text{(see figure 3.8)}$$

However, an adjustment of capital use to fulfil this condition is something we expect a profit maximising firm to achieve on its own. Hence, the use of capital need not be subsidised. In order to ensure the employment of $\bar{L}$ persons the firm has to be provided with an incentive to employ such a number of people. This is achieved by directly adjusting the terms for increasing the labour input, that is by subsidising labour inputs.

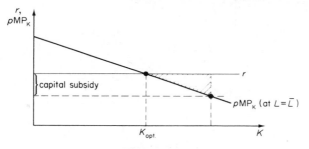

Figure 3.8

Specifically, the firm's unit cost of labour inputs p_L should be reduced by a subsidy S, so that the profit maximising behaviour of the firm

$$pMP_L = p\,\frac{\partial q}{\partial L} = p_L - S$$

leads to the employment of $\bar{L}$ persons.

Subsidising capital use would have meant establishing an incentive to substitute capital for labour at each level of output. In addition, it would tend to stimulate production. Hence, it is conceivable that a capital subsidy would have a positive net effect on employment. The conclusion in the preceding paragraph however, means that this kind of subsidy is more expensive for society; that is, it requires more capital than is optimal for attaining the given employment goal (see figure 3.8), and the returns on the extra amount of capital are below what it would be possible to achieve elsewhere in the economy. The result is a loss of output value equal to the shaded area in the figure. Thus, it is less efficient to subsidise capital use than to subsidise the employment of labour directly. This is an example of the important and rather obvious principle that the activity to be subsidised should be the one the government wishes to see increased.

3.2.3 Efficient Intertemporal Distribution Policy and the Level of Aggregate Investments

It is usually assumed that individuals are capable of determining their own optimal distribution between consumption today and consumption in the future. It is more dubious, however, to assume that another aspect

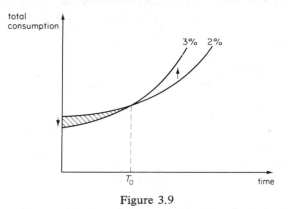

Figure 3.9

of intertemporal distribution, namely the distribution of consumption among generations, will be taken into account by the market itself. Generations not yet born are, of course, without political representation today and hence incapable of influencing today's division of income between consumption and investment. Therefore, so the argument goes, there are risks that the interests of future generations will be neglected by making today's consumption level 'too' high. On these grounds, today's government may feel an obligation to protect the interests of future generations and, if necessary, to increase the investment volume and thereby the growth of income and possibilities for future consumption.

The effects of a policy of stimulating investments in general is illustrated in figure 3.9. Given a situation in which total output capacity (GNP) and total consumption grow by 2 per cent a year, a certain increase in investments would raise the growth rate to 3 per cent a year. This means that generations after year T_0 may enjoy a higher consumption level than would otherwise have been possible. It also means that generations up to year T_0 have to make sacrifices equal to the shaded area in the figure.

In many countries, including those with a high standard of living, governments have growth targets that make it necessary to support the investment activity in the economy. As for industrialised countries, these targets can hardly be viewed as reflecting an ambition to provide future generations with an 'acceptable' standard of living. This is because these countries tend to have an automatic increase in GNP per capita, that is, a continuous increase in real consumption per capita without government intervention to support the level of investments. This means that today's level of consumption could be increased to some extent without forcing future generations to accept a standard of living lower than that of any previous generation.

The efforts to increase growth rates in real GNP in industrialised countries therefore seem to call for another motive than the one discussed so far. This motive may be found among factors such as national prestige and protection of future defence potentials. In fact, it seems likely that considerations of this kind make today's generation 'poor' in relation to future generations.

Now, if the policy objective is to protect the interests of future generations, the overall productive capacity (GNP) cannot be said to be the only relevant aspect to be taken into account. The future structure of productive capacity will also be important in this perspective since capacity for production of specific goods and services can never be transferred immediately—and sometimes not at all—to the production of other commodities. One aspect of this kind that has received a great deal of attention lately is the capacity to produce 'environmental services' in the future, that is to say, the capability of future society to provide opportunities for outdoor recreation in unspoiled natural surroundings, opportunities for living in a 'traditional' urban environment, etc. It is perfectly possible that the nation's present investment volume is 'unnecessarily' large in terms of maintaining at least today's level of material consumption for future generations, while at the same time certain kinds of investments such as 'investments in future environmental quality' are too small (that is, today's level of environmental degradation is too high) to give future generations today's opportunities for enjoying a high environmental quality.

A situation of this kind, if actually relevant, obviously means that today's investment structure is inefficient. By changing this structure, today's total investment volume could be reduced without reducing the standard of living for future generations below the present level; a large reduction in future capacity for material consumption could be compensated by a small increase in future environmental quality (small in terms of sacrifices today). That is to say, today's generation could consume more than is now the case if the investment structure were to be adjusted to match the expected structure of future demand.

3.2.4   Government Aid and Efficient Assistance to Poor Countries

In the three preceding sections we have dealt with various aspects of domestic income redistribution. We now intend to discuss efficiency aspects of measures aimed at changing international income distribution. Specifically, we address ourselves to the question of whether certain established forms of government aid to underdeveloped countries are efficient in promoting economic growth in recipient countries, that is whether a given 'sacrifice' on the part of the donor country would have a larger effect on development in recipient countries if aid forms were changed. This formulation of the problem means that we do not intend to discuss whether or not a given form of government aid is an efficient instrument for solving problems in the donor country, for example by increasing employment in certain sectors of the donor country.

Government aid to poor countries has often been criticised for having insignificant effects on development. This criticism usually involves one or more of the following three arguments.

(1) Private business investments in poor countries would be more efficient than government aid, primarily because projects would then be better adjusted to the production possibilities of recipient countries and, hence, would yield a higher rate of return on the efforts made.

(2) Too many government assistance projects fail. These failures could be avoided.

(3) Government aid has involved an unnecessarily high level of administrative costs.

Our aim in this section is not to determine whether or not criticism on these points is justified in particular instances. Instead, we intend to demonstrate that although government aid may appear to be inefficient, it can actually be found to be efficient given the special characteristics of development assistance. It is in this perspective that we now turn to examine the three critical remarks just mentioned.

(1) The view that government aid is less efficient than development aid in the form of private investments (read: than government subsidies to private foreign investments in poor countries) can be questioned in at least three respects. Firstly, unlike private firms, government agencies normally have to 'open their books' to the general public. Hence, it is much more difficult for government agencies than for private firms to keep individual investment failures quiet. In the long run this may easily give the impression that economic activity in the government sector is relatively less efficient even when its performance is equal to that of the private sector (*incomplete possibilities for comparison*).

Secondly, government projects usually encompass a greater number of targets (employment levels, labour training, etc.) than seems to be the case for private projects. The necessity of balancing several targets implies that high profits or similar one-dimensional targets relevant for private firms are not and should not be maximised when government projects are selected and designed. Hence, when comparisons between private and government projects are made with respect to profitability (whenever it is at all possible to make such comparisons) the government projects will appear to be less efficient (*irrelevant critieria for comparison*).

Finally, there is a large number of important activities, which for institutional or other reasons can only be administered by government agencies. This applies to a large extent to areas such as education, communications and health care. Efficient development aid requires extensive efforts also—and perhaps, primarily—in these areas. Private investment projects, to the extent they are conceivable (institutionally speaking) in this context, cannot of course be said to be more efficient than government projects in this case (*impossible comparisons*).

To sum up our objections to the argument that private investment projects are more efficient than direct government assistance, we conclude (a) that the development effects of certain government projects cannot be achieved in practice by private business and (b) that, whenever projects can be undertaken by either government or business, government assistance sometimes appears to be less efficient even when it is not.

(2) There is a widespread opinion that a large number of projects in government assistance programmes fail and that this is proof of inefficiency. As far as the observed frequency of project failures is concerned, this may once again be an illusion to a large extent. One reason for this is that many

successful projects are not reported by news media, essentially because information of this kind ('it turned out the way we thought it would') cannot be expected to be as interesting to the general public as the fiascos are. Thus, an overly negative impression of performance as a whole may easily develop.

We shall not, however, argue that it is an incorrect observation that a large number of government aid projects fail. Our point is instead that such an outcome is natural in this context and still *compatible* with efficiency. In other words, what we question is the value of 'failure frequency' as evidence of inefficiency in development aid.

First of all, we should ask what kind of comparison is intended, when it is argued that there is a high frequency of unsuccessful projects in government aid. If we regard the statement as the outcome of a comparison with similar projects in the growing and industrialised donor country, it must be pointed out that capital formation in the latter case is to a

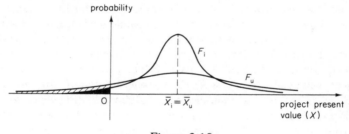

Figure 3.10

large extent a routine matter. Moreover, in the developed country there is normally better information about existing and future markets for factors of production and for output. By contrast, investments and similar projects in poor countries are carried out in a setting that is more or less completely unknown. In fact, this may be regarded as one of the characteristics of economic underdevelopment.

What we have just said may be expressed more formally in the following way. The probability distribution of possible outcomes of an average project in an industrialised country has a smaller variance than the corresponding distribution for a typical project in an underdeveloped country This means, for example, that if these two average projects had the same expected value ('most probable rate of return') the failure risk would be larger for the project in the underdeveloped country, failure being defined as, say, a negative present value of the project. (Compare the two shaded areas in figure 3.10 where F_i (F_u) is the probability distribution of outcomes $X_i(X_u)$ of an average investment project in the industrialised (underdeveloped) country and where $\bar{X}_i(\bar{X}_u)$ is the expected value of the project.)

It is certainly true that even in poor countries there are relatively safe projects, that is projects for which the variance of the probability distribution is small. A concentration of assistance programmes to such projects would of course reduce the number of 'failures'. At the same time, however, a policy of this kind would mean that the project selection in general would be confined to projects with relatively small expected values ($\bar{X}_u$). Hence, the overall effect of the assistance programme would decrease and so would the rate of development in the recipient country. Such a policy can hardly be in the interest of the recipient country. In fact, we may conclude that a large number of 'unsuccessful' projects is compatible with efficiency that is with a high development effect.

(3) The third point remains to be commented on. This is the often heard argument that an unnecessarily large part of government aid to poor countries is swallowed up by administrative costs. Now, as we have just pointed out, investments and other assistance projects are carried out in an essentially unknown economic environment. This means, of course, that extensive planning measures must be taken (by national or international institutions) in order to make it at all possible to undertake the projects. A crucial issue, then is whether a minimum level of such administrative measures can be expected to constitute an optimal level as well.

It is obvious that devoting more resources to the planning of projects in general would make the projects less likely to fail. It is also clear, however, that such measures would reduce the part of the budget that is actually transferred to the receiving country. This distribution problem is illustrated in figure 3.11 where the given aid budget is divided between A (expenditure on planning, control and other administrative activities) and T (resources actually transferred to the receiving countries) and where the estimated aggregate development effect is shown on the vertical axis. The curve in the figure indicates how the development effect varies with changes in the composition of A and T in the budget. As the curve is drawn here, the optimum composition is attained when $A = A_0$. The main point, however, is that there is no reason to believe that the minimum level of administrative costs—or any other savings in administrative costs below A_0—is compatible with efficiency.

In specific cases of aid to poor countries for which there is little
practical experience, the optimal level of administrative costs may be
quite high. The objective now is not only to achieve efficiency in current
aid activities but also to gain experience so that future development aid
can be planned more efficiently. Thus, today's assistance has an 'investment' or learning-by-doing aspect that should be observed when attempts
are made to determine the actual returns on administrative inputs and
the optimal level of administrative costs. For this reason alone, a high
ratio of administrative costs in government assistance as compared to
the usually more sporadic private investments in underdeveloped
countries (and to investments in the industrialised donor country, for
that matter) does not constitute a proof of inefficiency. Again, 'high'

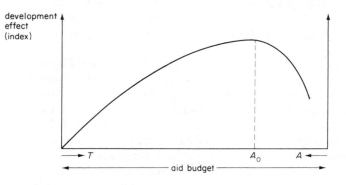

Figure 3.11

levels of administrative costs may be seen to be compatible with efficiency
in long-term government assistance programmes.

Summing up the arguments in this section, we have pointed out that
the validity of crucial arguments of alleged inefficiency in government
assistance to poor countries can be seriously questioned. It should be
stressed, however, that our remarks by no means constitute a proof of
the opposite argument that traditional assistance policy has been efficiently organised. The fact that a large number of project failures, a high
level of administrative costs, etc. can be seen to be compatible with
efficiency does not of course preclude the possibility that these figures
have been unnecessarily high. Our point is essentially that not only
government aid but also criticism of this aid should be confronted with
certain quality requirements.

3.2.5 Summary

We have dealt with four areas of distribution policy and found that all
of them involve efficiency aspects. This means not only that objective
analysis is feasible to some extent in this context—in spite of the fact
that targets of distribution policy concern subjective values—but also
that such an analysis aids in the attainment of distribution policy targets
regardless of their nature. In other words, we have studied a few examples
of the fact that efficiency can facilitate rather than obstruct the achieve-
ment of policy targets, irrespective of the shape of these goals and of the
actual values behind these goals.

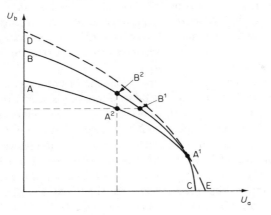

Figure 3.12

On a more formal level, we may summarise our presentation in the
preceding four sections in the following way. As before, let U_a and U_b
indicate the ranking of possible alternatives relevant for individuals a
and b, respectively. These two may represent persons living in the same
region, persons living in two different regions, persons belonging to two
different generations or persons from two different countries, one
developed and the other underdeveloped. Now, let us assume that distribution policy is aimed at a transfer from a to b. Using a certain type of
policy instrument—for example, traditional welfare policy, capital subsidies in depressed areas, measures to stimulate investments in general and
subsidies to private investments in underdeveloped countries, respectively
—the transfer would imply a shift, say, along the AC curve in figure 3.12
from A^1 to A^2. Now, by changing the policy instruments—for example,

to a negative income tax, to labour subsidies in depressed areas, to an adjustment of the investment structure and to government financial assistance, respectively—a higher level of efficiency might be attained. This, then, would be indicated by shifts along the BC curve in figure 3.12.

An increase in efficiency of this type could be used in various ways depending on the values behind the distribution goals. One possible example would be that the efficiency gain as a whole be allowed to remain with the 'donor' a, thus resulting in a final position of B^1. The opposite extreme would be to let the recipient b have the total gain, so that the final position would be at point B^2. These two examples indicate that a consensus on the choice of policy instruments can be obtained among individuals, despite vast differences in ideological views and values, with reference to the goals of distribution policy. These differences, in fact, refer to a separate issue, the *extent* to which the policy instruments should be used.

Against the background of the discussion in this chapter, the purpose of social-efficiency analysis can be seen to imply a search for policy instruments that can be used to reach a state of *maximum-feasible* efficiency. In terms of figure 3.12, this means that attempts are made to approach the DE curve as much as possible (in the relevant section 'north-east' of A^2). The DE curve, as we recall from figure 3.5, refers to the set of Pareto optima that can be attained, given the level of resources and technical know-how, but which may be infeasible in practice due to imperfections in, or negative side-effects of, available economic policy instruments†.

---

† It should be observed that the *feasible optima* described, say, by the BC curve in figure 3.12, are also kinds of Pareto optima since it is practically speaking, impossible to move from a point on that curve to a position preferred by both parties. These optima constitute the feasible or the so-called *second-best* Pareto optima. As follows from our discussion in chapter 1, these Pareto optima, however, do not meet the conditions for Pareto optimality as they were presented there; that is, they do not meet the conditions for what we may now call a *potential* (or 'first-best') Pareto optimum, described by the points on the DE curve in figure 3.12.

4. COST–BENEFIT ANALYSIS OF PUBLIC INVESTMENTS AND POLICY MEASURES

The purpose of this chapter is to demonstrate in more detail how the effects of government actions on the economy as a whole can be analysed and compiled to form a basis for decision-making. In this introductory section, conventional criteria for profitable business investments are used as a starting-point for deriving the so-called cost–benefit criterion for public investments and other public undertakings.

In elementary economic theory, the criterion for profitable investments implies that the discounted value (the present value) of all revenues(+) and costs(−) that accrue to the investing company should exceed zero. This criterion can, in most cases, be given an alternative formulation: that the internal rate of return on investment should exceed the discount rate of interest. Regardless of the formulation chosen, this criterion has limited relevance from the point of view of social efficiency.

Firstly, it presupposes that investments are justified only if they give rise to a financial surplus. This means, among other things, that profitable investments must have financial revenues, that is an inflow of payments. Secondly, this criterion covers only direct effects on the decision-maker (the investing company), not the external and other indirect effects of investments that are, or may be, relevant for the economy as a whole. Thirdly, market prices are used in calculating costs and revenues, even when these prices are irrelevant from the point of view of the economy as a whole.

Cost–benefit (CB) analysis, on the other hand, tries to take all the aspects mentioned in the preceding paragraph into account. Thus, it will be more comprehensive than the investment profitability calculations relevant from the point of view of the individual firm. The two types of calculation coincide only in the special case of a perfect market economy without external effects, public goods, decreasing cost industries, etc. (or where such a model can be regarded as a reasonable approximation of the real world), and where the government's concern is limited to attaining a state of social efficiency (Pareto optimality). CB analysis is also more general in the sense that it allows us to analyse the consequences of legislative changes, regulations and economic policy measures as well as those of ordinary investment projects.

Cost–benefit analysis is based on the existence of a policy goal of social efficiency, but it implies that projects (or other measures) are evaluated and accepted or rejected in accordance with the existence of other given policy goals as well. In general, the purpose of CB analysis is to achieve maximum-feasible efficiency subject to constraints, which reflect policy objectives concerning, for example, the income distribution of the economy. It is quite possible, however, to use other formulations such as a maximum redistribution to a particular income group subject to a constraint concerning efficiency and other relevant targets. As these alternatives can be shown to produce identical results for a given set of basic policy objectives, we may also use the first-mentioned 'traditional' formulation.

Given a project and given the social environment in which the project, if accepted, would be carried out, the project can be found to have effects in a number (n) of dimensions and during a number of periods. Denoting the effect of dimension i in period t by X_{ti}, the total effects of the project can be listed as follows:

$$\text{Period 1:} \quad x_{11} \ x_{12} \ \ldots x_{1n}$$
$$\text{Period 2:} \quad x_{21} \ x_{22} \ \ldots x_{2n}$$
$$\cdot$$
$$\cdot$$
$$\cdot$$

In order to be able to ascertain the total social impact of these effects, an attempt is made to evaluate each of them in money terms ($\pounds p_{ti}$), to discount the resulting sum of values for each period at some rate of interest ($r_t \geq 0$) and to calculate the present value of the project. In the following presentation, the positive effects ($X_{ti} > 0$) will be called the benefits and the negative effects ($X_{ti} < 0$) the costs of the project. Those effects that cannot be defined or evaluated in a meaningful way are neglected for the time being (see section 4.6).

The cost–benefit criterion for a socially profitable project can now be formulated. The criterion implies that the present value of benefits and costs be positive, that is, that

$$\sum_{t=1}^{\infty} \frac{\sum\limits_{i=1}^{n} p_{ti}x_{ti}}{(1 + r_1)(1 + r_2)(1 + r_3) \cdots (1 + r_t)} > 0$$

subject to one or more constraints, for example, $x_{13} \geqslant \bar{x}_{13}$, $\sum\limits_{i=1}^{k} p_{2i}x_{2i} = 0$,

or with a general formulation for each constraint, $F(x_{11}, x_{12} \ldots;$ $p_{11}, p_{12} \ldots) = 0$. (See section 4.4.1 for concrete examples of such constraints.)

If there is only one way of designing each project, the problem will simply be to select those projects that have a positive present value and that meet the given constraints. However, if projects can be designed in alternative ways, then the optimal design of each project has to be determined. The result will be the design that maximises the present value of the project. Given perfect divisibility (that is, variability of the size) of the project, this additional requirement implies that inputs of factors of production into the project should be increased up to the point where the marginal effect on the present value is zero for each factor, provided that the marginal return on each factor is decreasing.

Before proceeding, we shall simplify the approach just described in two respects. Firstly, we should observe that, as a rule, it is not possible to calculate a specific discount rate for each future period. Nor is it normally possible to estimate the effects that will appear far in the future. For these reasons, we shall have to be satisfied with using a constant discount rate (r) and a time horizon (T), which is chosen more or less arbitrarily. Hence, the CB criterion can be reformulated as follows

$$\sum_{t=1}^{T} \frac{\sum\limits^{n} p_{ti}x_{ti}}{(1 + r)^t} > 0$$

subject to the given constraints.

The principal problems of CB analysis may be discussed under the following five headings:

(1) *The Quantification Problem.* How should the costs and benefits, X_{ti}, of the project be identified and measured in physical terms?

(2) *The Valuation Problem.* How should the socially relevant values of the physical effects of the projects, that is the p_{ti}, be determined?

(3) *The Discounting Problem.* How should the discount rate (r) relevant for the economy as a whole be determined?

(4) *The Constraints Problem.* How should the constraints on project design (if relevant) and on project approval be determined and formulated?

(5) *The Uncertainty Problem.* How can we allow for the fact that future effects, weights (prices), discount rates and constraints are often impossible to determine with certainty?

4.1   The Quantification Problem

According to what principles should the items of social costs and benefits that arise from a project under CB analysis be identified? As we indicated in the introductory section, it is not sufficient to take into consideration only the effects that accrue to the investing company or government agency. It must also be observed that the project may have effects elsewhere in the economy. If the project gives rise to negative or positive *external effects* (for a definition of this term, see section 2.1), these effects should be taken into account as cost and benefit items, respectively. For example, the construction of a hydroelectric power station may create external effects by destroying existing recreation areas (a negative effect) and/or it may even out the flow of water to downstream power plants and, hence, make it possible for these plants to increase their power production (a positive effect).

Now, it should be stressed that all indirect effects of a project do not necessarily have to be included among its social costs and benefits. Specifically, the quantitative effects via the market mechanism should in general not be taken into account (see note 1, page 24). For example, increased output from companies owing to the purchase of inputs for the project under study, can be neglected as long as these purchases are made at constant prices equal to marginal social costs. (The case in which purchases are large enough to affect prices will be dealt with later on.) To take another example, a regional increase in service output, etc., arising from the project's being carried out or, more specifically, from the purchases made by workers who have moved in from another area, is matched by a reduction in service output of about the same size in the areas from which the workers have moved. As long as these shifts occur without any changes in social costs, they can be neglected.

In the last example, the project could be seen to give rise to *income transfers* from service firms in one area to similar firms in another. A redistribution of this kind may of course be of interest to policy makers. If so, this aspect should not, however, be observed in the present context; it will be taken care of by introducing a distribution policy constraint on the selection of investment projects, not by letting it affect the present value of the individual project.

To conclude, the selection of cost items to be included in the CB calculation of a project is governed by the principle of whether or not the item involves using up real resources. Similarly, benefit items are effects of the project that imply an addition to real resources (in the form of commodities).

4.2   The Valuation Problem

We shall now tackle a somewhat more difficult problem than that of identifying the cost and benefit items of a project. For simplicity we assume to begin with that the project under study, if undertaken, would materialise in a perfect market economy and in a setting in which no prices are influenced other than those of the commodity and factor markets that are directly affected. Moreover, throughout this section the actual income distribution of the economy is assumed to be in line with the distribution goals of the government. This assumption enables us to identify consumer valuations with valuations of society as a whole (as expressed by the policy objectives of the government).

4.2.1   *Valuation of Benefit Items*
Consumer goods.   Provided that the consumer goods or services the project would produce are sold at marginal cost prices (see page 15), revenues in accordance with these prices may be a sufficient basis for evaluating the output of the project. For many government investment projects, however, this calculation of benefits is insufficient. When benefits evaluated at marginal cost prices turn out to fall short of the total costs of the project, the project may still be worthwhile from the point of view of the economy as a whole (see section 2.3). This is the case in which the *consumers' total willingness to pay* can be shown to exceed total costs. It can be demonstrated that, under certain fairly general conditions, the consumers' willingness to pay approximately equals the area under the demand curve, that is to say, the financial revenues pq_0 plus the shaded area, the so-called *consumer's surplus,* in

figure 4.1. (See appendix 2 for a definition of consumers' surplus.) However, in practice it is often quite difficult to estimate this total value of the project output. The following methods are conceivable. In the first two, an attempt is made to change prices so that the financial revenues approach the consumers' total maximum willingness to pay. The third method simply amounts to finding out whether the willingness to pay is sufficiently large to cover the costs of the project.

(1) *Price differentiation* (different consumers pay different prices) allows financial revenues to exceed pq_0. In the special case in which

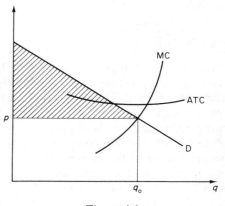

Figure 4.1

perfect discrimination is feasible the financial revenues could coincide with the maximum willingness to pay. This solution, however, is compatible with efficiency only if each consumer would buy the same quantity of the commodity now as when prices were equal to marginal costs (for example, as in the case of commodities of which each consumer buys one and only one unit).

(2) *Two-part tariffs,* according to which consumers pay a licence or subscription fee in order to obtain access to the market, as well as a (marginal cost) price for each unit of the commodity. In this case, it is usually impossible for revenues to come very close to the maximum willingness to pay.

(3) If a hypothetical equilibrium price above average costs can be shown to exist it follows that the willingness to pay must exceed total

costs and hence, that the project must be socially worthwhile. The maximal social net benefits will of course be attained at a larger output and at a price equal to marginal costs, that is at q_o. It should be observed that the existence of a hypothetical price, capable of giving a financial profit, is a sufficient, but not a necessary condition for social profitability (see page 39).

(4) If none of these three methods is applicable, there remains the possibility of direct inquiry into the consumers' willingness to pay. However, if consumers are not called upon to make payments in relation to their stated willingness to pay, that is, if they are asked only about their hypothetical willingness to pay, we cannot be sure that they will reveal their true preferences for the commodity (see page 35).

A special case of marginal-cost pricing that gives rise to a financial deficit occurs when marginal costs are zero (for example, uncongested roads and bridges). A zero price, however, may be socially efficient even when marginal costs are positive. This is so when costs of collecting a price (collection costs) are significant, as in the case of congested streets. Here, the difficulties of estimating the maximum willingness to pay are even more pronounced, since methods (1)–(3) are ruled out.

Producer goods.   What has been said so far applies to cases in which a project would produce a commodity for direct consumer use. If the output consists of goods delivered to producers, then, given the assumptions of a perfect market economy and provided prices do not change, the market value of output gives an adequate estimate of the benefit side of the project. This value is shown by the shaded area in figure 4.2 where project output appears as an addition to total supply of a certain producer good[†].

Now, if prices were to change[‡] so that the output of the project, say a hydroelectric power station, gave rise to a reduction in the price of electrical power, we would once again run into a case in which the social benefits of the project exceed its financial revenues. Here, we may

[†] The case described in figures 4.2 and 4.3 can be explained as follows: The increased supply of q_p due to the introduction of the project under study has such a small effect on the price p_p that the price can be viewed as constant when calculating project benefits. The price change, however, is significant enough to explain why the buyers of q_p (= the producers of q_c) increase their purchases in the amount of the project's addition to total output. In other words, the constancy of the price at p_p is to be regarded as an approximation of a small price change.

[‡] The discussion of this case is relatively complex and may be omitted without serious consequences for the line of argument.

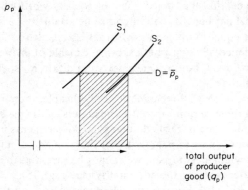

Figure 4.2

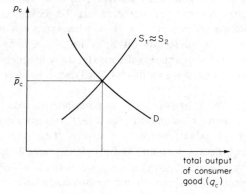

Figure 4.3

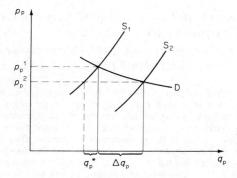

Figure 4.4.

distinguish between two alternative situations, (1) in which the equilibrium price p_c in the power consuming sector c (here assumed to be an industry producing consumer goods) is not affected (see figures 4.4 and 4.5) and (2) in which this price is reduced (figures 4.6 and 4.7).

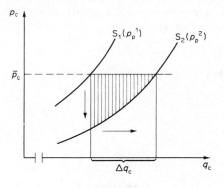

Figure 4.5

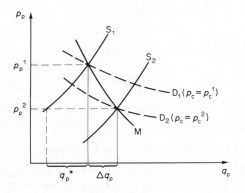

Figure 4.6

(1) In case 1 we depart from the supply curve S_1, which prevails at the original price of the producer goods, p_p^1 (see figure 4.4). In the new equilibrium position of the economy, p_p will have fallen to p_p^2 and sector c will have adjusted its output by Δq_c to the new set of equilibrium prices, p_p^2 and $\bar{p}_c$, the latter being constant in this case. This output change is achieved by means of an increase of input q_p by Δq_p and of other inputs q_L by Δq_L, the price of these factors p_L, being assumed

to be constant. The maximum willingness to pay for this addition to output in sector c, which is the same as the value of Δq_p, thus equals

$$\bar{p}_c \Delta q_c - \bar{p}_L \Delta q_L$$

This expression can be seen to exceed $p_p{}^2 \Delta q_p$ (the sector output change measured at the new price) since the profits arising from the adjustment of output in sector c equal

$$\bar{p}_c \Delta q_c - \bar{p}_L \Delta q_L - p_p{}^2 \Delta q_p > 0$$

(see the shaded area in figure 4.5).

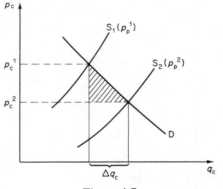

Figure 4.7

(2) In case 2, the price of the consumer commodity is also influenced, being reduced from $p_c{}^1$ to $p_c{}^2$. The value of Δq_p in this case is equal to

$$p_c{}^2 \Delta q_c + \text{(the shaded area in figure 4.7)} - \bar{p}_L \Delta q_L$$

This value also exceeds $p_p{}^2 \Delta q_p$. (Note that $p_p{}^2$ and Δq_p in case 1 exceed p_p^2 and Δq_p in case 2, given the initial equilibrium position and the change from S_1 to S_2 in both cases. It should also be noted that curve M in figure 4.6 is a curve that combines equilibrium points, that is equilibrium combinations of q_p and p_p. A first point on this curve is given by the intersection of S_1 and the demand curve D_1 relevant for $p_c = p_c{}^1$. A second point is given by the intersection of S_2 and D_2 relevant for $p_c = p_c{}^2$.

In order to estimate the *total* social gross benefits of the project, the analysis has to be carried one step further. In both cases the effect of the project on equilibrium output q_p consists of two components:

(a) the increase of q_p (the value of which we have just defined) and (b) a substitution for the part of original output (q_p*) that was supplied by other producers at the original price p_p^1 but not supplied by them at the final price p_p^2 after our project has been introduced. The value of the latter component is as equal to the costs that these other producers had for the volume q_p*, that is costs which society now will avoid. This cost reduction together with the value of Δq_p thus describes the total gross benefits of the project to be weighed against the total social costs of the project.

Positive external effects It seems natural to include possible positive external effects among the benefits of the project. The valuation problem here is, in principle, identical to those already discussed. That is to say, positive external effects on consumers and producers should be valued according to the maximum willingness to pay of the recipients of these effects. On a practical level, this estimation problem may be quite difficult, since effects of this kind—by definition—are not traded on a market and hence cannot be valued at market determined prices (see section 2.1). Estimation will, of course, become even more complicated if price reductions and hence changes in consumers' surplus occur as a consequence of positive external effects on producers.

4.2.2 Valuation of Project Costs
Provided that no prices in the perfect market economy are affected by the purchase of project inputs or by negative external effects caused by the project, no particular complications arise when estimating the cost items of the project. On the other hand, if the price of a factor does change, the resource use of the project must be calculated as equal to the total social costs for the increased factor supply caused by the introduction of the project, plus the value of reduced output in the rest of the economy due to increased factor prices. In other words, we obtain a valuation problem similar to that discussed in the preceding section on producer goods. It should be observed, however, that in case the project net value turns out to be positive with costs estimated at *ex post* prices (alternatively, negative with costs estimated at *ex ante,* that is, original prices) it is quite sufficient to use these prices.

What we have just said can be illustrated by reference to figure 4.8. Owing to the introduction of our project, demand for factor q_L is assumed to increase by ΔD. As a consequence, the equilibrium factor price will increase from p_L^1 to p_L^2. Now, as indicated, social costs for

ΔD are made up of two components, reflecting the fact that two different opportunity costs are involved. One component is the value of output reduction elsewhere owing to the reduced factor inputs there as a consequence of the price increase; the other is the minimum payments required for additions to the total supply of q_L. The resulting total costs for ΔD, then, can be shown to be (approximately) equal to the area under the original demand curve and the supply curve, respectively, as indicated in the figure. With the costs for ΔD now given, it is evident that a calculation at the *ex post* price $p_L{}^2$, would give an overestimate and a calculation at the *ex ante* price $p_L{}^1$, would give an underestimate of the true social costs of the project.

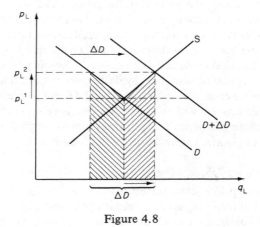

Figure 4.8

4.2.3   Many Projects

What has been said about the valuation problem so far concerns the individual independent project. From the point of view of the economy as a whole, all investment projects are potentially relevant for cost–benefit analysis. In the real-world mixed economy, however, there exists an 'institutional constraint' by which certain projects are 'handed over' to the private sector and to the investment criteria that prevail there[†]. The fact that the government has direct control over a large part of the

† As an alternative to public CB-analysis of all investment projects, general economic policy measures can be used to adjust prices and interest rates that confront private companies. In this way, known private investment criteria can be made to produce the same set of projects that a general CB-approach would have brought about.

economy and, hence, over a large number of investment projects still remains to be taken into account.

The fact that several projects can be undertaken more or less simultaneously will have a bearing on the valuation problem in the sense that the likelihood of prices in the relevant factor and commodity markets remaining unchanged will be reduced. In accordance with what has been said above, it will now be necessary to make forecasts of the price changes that result from the introduction of a whole set of projects. To the extent that many projects affect the same markets, these price changes may turn out to have significant repercussions on the design, ranking and final choice of individual projects.

It should be added that, when several projects have costs and/or benefits that are mutually interdependent, the individual projects must be compared not only with one another but also with different combinations of projects. Otherwise, an optimal set of projects cannot be determined.

4.2.4   Imperfect Market Prices

We shall now withdraw the simplifying assumption made so far that market prices are perfect, that is that they correctly reflect consumer valuations and opportunity costs. The problem of imperfect market prices may be a limited one, in the sense that for the purpose of CB calculations such prices may have to be subjected to minor adjustments only. Or, it may be extensive enough to jeopardise a meaningful application of CB analysis altogether. With respect to the latter case, it has been said that if market prices are allowed to deviate substantially from opportunity costs and consumer valuations, this must be interpreted as a consequence of the fact that the efficiency objective (which CB analysis traditionally as well as in this presentation has been based upon) is either absent or assigned a low priority. Thus, under these circumstances, it would follow that CB analysis, as we have formulated it here, is irrelevant or uncalled for. But from another point of view, this observation can be taken to imply that, whenever CB analysis as formulated here is considered to be relevant, the deviations between market prices and accounting prices for CB calculations cannot be expected to exist to such an extent that this kind of analysis is rendered superfluous or basically misleading.

Against this background, our task will simply be to describe how imperfect market prices have to be adjusted before they can be used in CB analysis. We distinguish the following three reasons why market prices

deviate from the relevant accounting prices (or shadow prices): (1)
imperfect competition, (2) market disequilibrium, (3) non-efficiency
based taxes and subsidies.

(1) Imperfect competition.   This normally implies that the buyers'
price exceeds marginal costs (see the monopoly case shown in figure 4.9).
Provided that marginal costs correctly reflect opportunity costs, marginal
costs instead of actual market prices should be used when estimating
project purchases from firms under imperfect competition. However,
the provision that marginal costs reflect opportunity costs is hardly
fulfilled when imperfect competition and other forms of market imper-

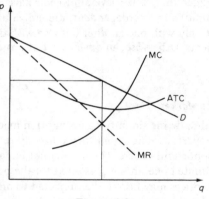

Figure 4.9

fections prevail in large parts of the economy. In this case, it may be
necessary to calculate relevant shadow prices from a more or less complete model of the local or national economy.

When calculating project benefits from sales of producer goods to
consumer-good producing firms under imperfect competition, the market
prices of the consumer goods should be used as a basis for shadow price
calculations, provided that these market prices reflect consumer valuations.
When project sales go to firms manufacturing producer goods, calculation
of project benefits should still be based on consumer valuations of the
ultimate output of consumer goods. In complex cases of this kind, a complete model of the local or national economy may once again be called for.

(2) Market disequilibrium.   In a situation of permanent disequilibrium,
it is usually impossible to use the market price for CB calculations. To

show this, we shall observe in turn the two cases of market prices above and below the equilibrium level (a and b), respectively. Moreover, we shall observe the effects of the project on the buyer side (case I) as well as on the seller side (case II) of such markets.

Case Ia. A market price above the equilibrium level (see p_2 in figure 4.10) implies that the market price exceeds marginal costs. (There are exceptions, however, where parts of the sales 'happen' to stem from the least efficient producers whose marginal costs approximately equal p_2.) In evaluating project purchases on such a market, marginal costs should be employed, provided they reflect opportunity costs of the resource use. A shadow price below the market price (or wage rate) may also be required for workers hired for the project, whenever they could not

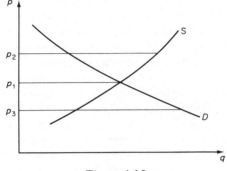

Figure 4.10

otherwise be employed at current market rates. It should be noted, however, that it is often very difficult to forecast the length of the period during which the employees can be taken to be without alternative job opportunities and during which the low original shadow price should be used.

Case Ib. Now, assume instead that the market price for a factor is below equilibrium (that is, that the factor is rationed) and that the introduction of the project leads to other buyers being driven out of the market. In this case, it is the value of the alternative use to which these buyers would have put the factors that determines the appropriate accounting price for the project inputs in question.

Case IIa–b. We now turn to the case where the project directly or indirectly involves selling products on a disequilibrium market. When prices on this market are above the equilibrium level, that is, when there is excess supply, the value of project sales is correctly determined by the costs eliminated among those producers who are no longer able to sell (part of) their output owing to the intrusion of the project. In the opposite case where prices are below the equilibrium level (excess demand) project output value is equal to the value assigned to it by the consumers of the addition to market output.

If, in any of the disequilibrium cases discussed, the relative size of project output or project inputs is large enough to affect the level of marginal costs or consumer valuations, respectively, the resulting changes in shadow prices should be taken into account as we indicated above for changes in perfect market prices.

(3) Non-efficiency-based taxes and subsidies. The government may use taxes and subsidies in order to make market prices reflect social costs, for example in the presence of external effects. If these attempts are successful, market prices that include these taxes or subsidies should be used as accounting prices for calculations of project costs and project benefits. If, on the other hand, taxes and subsidies do not have the said purpose (as is usually the case for, say, energy taxes and agricultural subsidies), it may be necessary to deduct them altogether.

Let us take an example. Say that in a perfect market economy an excise tax has been levied on a particular commodity (such as fuel) used in a project under study. If that commodity is available at a constant market price, its real social costs will equal the market price less the tax; that is it will equal the marginal costs of production. The reason is, of course, that abstention from buying these inputs would mean that resources, in the amount of the marginal costs, need not be used up. In the opposite case, however, if commodity supply were constant, the project would use inputs that otherwise would be used elsewhere in the economy and hence the inputs should be valued at market prices, that is including the tax. As we can see, correct calculations on this point also involve establishing the relevant opportunity costs (see the analysis of figure 4.8 for the two extreme cases of a horizontal and a vertical supply curve, respectively).

4.3   The Discounting Problem

4.3.1   Reasons for Discounting Future Costs and Benefits
Future revenue and future costs are discounted because (1) resources that are not used up in the production of commodities for immediate

consumption can be employed in investment projects yielding a return that exceeds the value of inputs and, (2) simultaneously consumers require compensation for reducing their consumption today in favour of consumption at a later date. Thus, given a capability as well as a willingness to exchange commodities at one date for a larger volume of commodities at a later date, a price or an exchange rate will emerge between values today and values in the future. This exchange rate, which reveals a rate of interest or rate of discount, can then be used to translate (discount) future costs and benefits to corresponding values today.

4.3.2   The Applicability of a Market Rate of Interest

In a perfect market economy, a uniform rate of interest is established for each period of time, reflecting the valuations of the individuals living and trading during that period as well as the profitability of available investment opportunities. Even if this type of economy did exist in reality, we could still not be sure that the resulting market interest rate would be relevant for calculating the present social value of future cost and benefit flows. The government may attach more weight to the economic welfare of future generations than the present generation, as manifested by its market behaviour, is automatically willing to do. If this is the case, a rate of discount lower than the market rate of interest should be used, implying that future net values are given more weight and that investments are made to appear more attractive than at the market rate of interest. At the same time, it is evident that the present generation, even when acting on purely egotistical grounds, may bring about an income distribution over time that meets the requirements of the government (see section 3.2.3). In that case, the market rate of interest of the perfect market economy would be an adequate rate of discount for all investment projects.

4.3.3   Market Imperfections

If we now observe that imperfections of the type discussed in section 4.2.4 may exist, the relevance of a market rate of interest for CB calculations will be more uncertain. By a procedure similar to the one we used earlier, the probable effects of disequilibrium, imperfect competition, etc., on various markets, including the credit market now have to be estimated in order to calculate the deviation between the actual and the perfect market rate of interest. Further complications may arise if there are political constraints, for example, in the form of disagreements between different branches of government. Such disagreements may concern (a) the size of the sector where CB calculations are to be made, so that investments in this sector are not allowed to be increased up to the point where returns on marginal projects would equal returns on marginal projects in the rest of the economy; or (b) the size of the total investment volume of the economy, so that this volume is kept from reaching the level desired by the executive branch of the government (provided that we base our analysis on the valuations of that body).

Point (b)—the effects of a constraint on the volume of total investments—is illustrated in a simplified form in figures 4.11–4.13. In figure

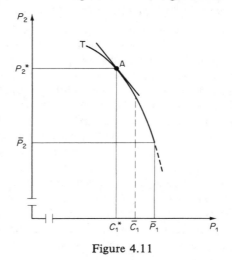

Figure 4.11

4.11, the total output of the economy in period 1 is given by $\bar{P}_1$. By investing a part of this output, the output in period 2 can be raised above $\bar{P}_2$ in accordance with the transformation curve T. Now, assuming that the executive branch of the government prefers point A on the transformation curve, that is to say, a combination of consumption 'today' equal to C_1^*, and output 'tomorrow' equal to P_2^*, the desired investment volume would equal $\bar{P}_1 - C_1^*$. The marginal rate of transformation at point A, which equals 1 plus the return on marginal investments at that point, would then also express the social marginal rate of time preference (SMT) between consumption in period 1 and feasible consumption in period 2 (see section 1.5). Now, if the market rate of interest (r_m) deviated from the return on marginal investments (i) at point A

(i = SMT − 1), this point could not be attained when investments are made up to the point where $i = r_m$. Thus, as long as r_m deviates from SMT − 1, the market rate of interest will be unsuitable as a rate of discount for investments, given a total volume of investments equal to

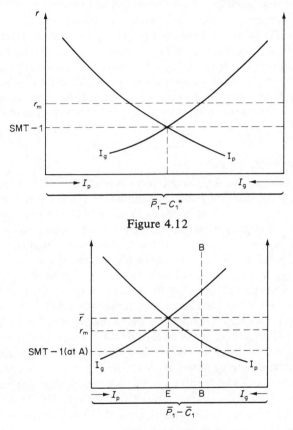

Figure 4.12

Figure 4.13

$\bar{P}_1 - C_1^*$. This situation is shown in figure 4.12, where the total volume of investments is divided between private investment projects (I_p) and public investment projects (I_g), both of which are ordered according to their rates of return from the left and from the right, respectively.

Now, having discussed the possible relevance of a market rate of interest when total investments in the economy are allowed to increase up to the desired level, let us assume that, for one reason or another, the total investment volume is given and equal to a *less than* optimal level, such as $\bar{P}_1 - \bar{C}_1$ in figures 4.11 and 4.13. In this case, neither the market rate of interest nor the social rate of marginal time preference (at point A or at the constrained investment level) can be expected to provide a rate of discount relevant for public investment calculations. The optimal allocation of the investment volume between I_p and I_g is attained at E in figure 4.13, that is, where returns on marginal projects in both sectors are identical (compare figure 4.12). Obviously, this optimal allocation calls for a rate of discount for government projects equal to $\bar{r}$, the rate of return on investments in the optimal position, and this value need not coincide with the market rate of interest in the presence of market imperfections.

4.3.4   Sensitivity Analysis

There has been considerable disagreement among economists as to the proper rate of discount for public investments in specific real-world situations. Proposals have varied over a range as wide as 3 per cent to 12 per cent, although nowadays a majority seems to have settled on values in the region of 8 per cent. Given this variety of opinion, it seems appropriate at this point to introduce an instrument of great importance for CB analysis in the presence of uncertainty. By estimating the net benefits of projects at different levels of discount rates, it is possible to ascertain the extent to which project outcomes are sensitive to differences in this respect. Sometimes it turns out that a project remains profitable or unprofitable regardless of the level of discount rate in the relevant interval and in these cases, of course, the choice of discount rate becomes unimportant. It should be noted, however, that in many cases, project profitability proves to be sensitive even to small changes in discount rates. In fact, CB analysis often concerns projects with effects that appear far into the future and, for obvious reasons, the choice of discount rate is likely to play a decisive role in such cases.

4.4   The Constraints Problem

As we have pointed out earlier, we have adhered to the traditional approach and based our presentation of CB analysis on a foundation of social efficiency. As is well known, however, political values may be attached to many aspects other than efficiency. We now turn to a discussion of the consequences of multidimensional targets and begin by observing government objectives with respect to income distribution.

4.4.1 Distribution Constraints

In practice, public investment projects may imply a redistribution of income among groups or individuals. This occurs even though a positive net benefit value of a project in itself means that benefits are large enough to compensate all who might lose as a consequence of the project. Moreover, in a world in which redistribution measures that are neutral with respect to efficiency do not exist (see chapter 3), public investment projects may be a practical way of achieving a desired change in income distribution. Given the existence of policy goals with respect to income distribution, investment projects will thus have to be subjected to a test of whether their distributive effects are compatible with these goals. One way of doing this is to introduce a constraint on the CB calculation of projects. Such a constraint may take the form of, for example, a minimum level for wages to labour employed, a minimum number of people employed, a minimum level of the increase in total incomes for a particular group or a minimum level of services provided free or for given low prices to people in the region where the investment is made.

Constraints of this type, regardless of their actual form, are not related to isolated projects but, in principle at least, to all public investment projects. This wide coverage is necessary in order for the constraints to be fulfilled in the most efficient way, that is, with a minimum loss of social efficiency given certain distribution goals.

The distribution goals can be expected to be revised over time as a result of observations about efficiency losses incurred in the process of satisfying a given set of constraints. But, to achieve overall social efficiency in this process, other and more direct means of income redistribution would have to be taken into consideration (see section 3.2.5)[†].

---

† In principle, income distribution aspects can be taken into account in CB analysis by adjusting project accounting prices instead of adding constraints on the maximisation of project net benefits. For example, benefit items accruing to particular groups whose incomes the government wants to support (say, the farm population in certain regions) may be given a higher weight than other benefit items. In practice, however, this more subtle approach will probably have to be replaced by the simpler and, perhaps more informative, constraint approach (although its effects are the same).

4.4.2 Budget Constraints

As we pointed out earlier (in section 4.3.3), there may be political
reasons for keeping the volume of public investments below a level at
which all projects with a positive present value can be carried out. (The
socially inefficient investment distribution in the economy that results
from an investment constraint of this kind is illustrated by line B in
figure 4.13.) In other cases, a conscious objective of restricting public
investments may be absent but a budget constraint may nevertheless
be present due to imperfect exchange of information between branches
of the government or to institutional inflexibility of one kind or
another. Such constraints may refer to specific parts of the government
sector such as certain types of projects or certain kinds of expenditures.
We limit our discussion, however, to the case of a constraint on the total
volume of public investments.

Since the investment budget is the scarce factor, the problem is
reduced to that of finding a maximum return (sum of net benefits) on
the given investment volume. Looking at the case in which investment
decisions in the public sector are decentralised to separate and independent government agencies, we may note, first of all, that optimal investment criteria in the absence of budget constraints imply that projects
with a positive present value should be carried out, with each project
being so designed that the return on a marginal increase in investment
costs is zero (see page 93). Now, if there exists an effective constraint
on investment resources, investments should be allocated among government agencies in such a way that (the now strictly positive) returns on
marginal investments in each field are equalised. Formally speaking, the
given total investment resources $\bar{K}$ should be allocated so that the investment budget for each field j, K_j, equalises dB_j/dK_j for all j, where B_j is
the net benefits of investments in field j (see $K_j^{(2)}$ in figure 4.14 for the
case of two agencies only).

Now, an allocation of this kind cannot be achieved directly unless all
projects in each field are known to the central authority. But if they are
known, decentralisation of investment decisions is obviously superfluous.
In reality, it is not efficient to collect complete information of this kind
(even if it were feasible) at the top level of government. Hence, a process
of successive approximations of the allocation of investment resources
has to be envisaged, starting from a preliminary and more or less arbitrary
division of the total investment budget (see $K_j^{(1)}$ in figure 4.14). After
each agency has calculated its dB_j/dK_j at a preliminary $\bar{K}_j$ and reported

its findings back to the central authority, investment resources will be reduced for agencies where dB_j/dK_j is low and transferred to agencies where returns on marginal investments are above average. These reallocations are carried out as long as time permits or up to the point at which an acceptable (somehow defined) degree of equality of returns on marginal investments has been achieved.

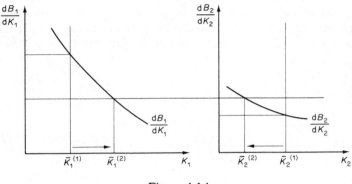

Figure 4.14

4.5   The Uncertainty Problem

So far we have treated the problems of CB analysis essentially as if project effects, accounting prices and constraints could be known with certainty. This information is, of course, often impossible to obtain, especially for projects with effects far in the future. In fact, not even effects in the immediate future—the investment costs of projects—can always be known with certainty.

4.5.1   Uncertain Project Effects and Accounting Prices

Provided that the government can be regarded as having a time-horizon of several years during which it undertakes a large number of investment projects in many separate fields, these investment projects can be treated as essentially independent of one another. Hence, we can anticipate that some projects will turn out worse and some better than their expected outcomes. In fact, according to the law of large numbers, we can expect that the negative and the positive 'surprises' would tend to cancel. Moreover, under the given circumstances (that is, a large number of independent projects) it is generally correct to rank projects according to their

expected outcomes only, regardless of the risk involved in each project
(that is, the variance of probability distributions of project outcomes)[†].

To be specific, let us compare two projects, A and B. The outcome
of project A is assumed to be (approximately) known while the effects
of project B and their corresponding weights can only be characterised
by estimated probability distributions. For simplicity, we assume that
the given probability distributions are not influenced by (additional)
expenditures on information gathering. The investment criterion just
mentioned implies here that the known outcome of project A should
be compared with the expected value of the outcome of the uncertain

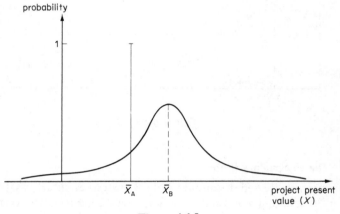

Figure 4.15

project B (see $\bar{X}_A$ and $\bar{X}_B$, respectively, in figure 4.15). This rule obviously
differs from the risk-averting behaviour we expect to be common among
private enterprises with only a few investment projects and with projects,
which are dependent on one another and/or on the same factors. A risk
averter prefers a risky project (B) to one with a known outcome (A) only
if the expected value of B is deemed to exceed the outcome of A by a
sufficiently large (subjectively determined) margin.

Unfortunately, far from all project outcomes can be characterised by
a well-defined probability distribution, and still fewer are known with
certainty. In those cases where not even the expected value can be determined with reasonable accuracy, the ranking of investment projects once

[†] For certain exceptions to this rule see Arrow and Lind, 'Uncertainty and the
Evaluation of Public Investment Decisions', *American Economic Review*, June 1970.

again becomes a problem. Should the 'degree' of uncertainty or ignorance with respect to project outcomes be taken into account or not? Once we imagine wide differences among projects in this regard, it is obvious that the answer must be yes. But it is perhaps equally obvious that there cannot be any specific and generally valid rules for how such considerations should be made. In less complex cases, an unambiguous verdict on project profitability can be arrived at on the basis of a sensitivity analysis, that is, by varying uncertain project effects (or their prices) within conceivable intervals (see section 4.3.4). But more often, perhaps, decision makers will be forced to rely on pure 'Fingerspitzgefühl'. In some cases, however, a possible escape may present itself in the form of postponing investment decisions to a later date, especially when there is reason to believe that ignorance will decrease over time. This often applies to projects using new technology—new kinds of nuclear power plants may be a case in point.

A special case of importance in this context involves projects the costs or benefits of which become increasingly more uncertain the farther into the future they occur. One suggested approach here is to assign lower weights to distant annual net benefits by a progressively higher rate of discount. It should be noted that this kind of an arrangement primarily affects project designs and has only a secondary influence on the choice among projects to the extent that projects vary with respect to their optimum time distribution of annual net benefits. Similar effects are obtained by the alternative approach of simply omitting project effects after a given future date. This approach is particularly relevant when uncertainty about project net benefits rises sharply after some period of time. An indiscriminate application of this approach may, however, have severe consequences, since for instance, negative long-term effects on the environment would thus be overlooked.

4.5.2   Uncertain Future Discount Rates and Constraints

As we have pointed out, discount rates and constraints refer in principle to all projects. Thus, if an adjustment in these respects is called for because of uncertainty about the future, it will affect public investment decisions in general.

If it is assumed that discount rates and/or constraints grow more uncertain over time, it has been suggested that future discount rates be gradually raised above the expected value and that constraints be gradually tightened. In the particular case where it is assumed that

future budget constraints will be drastically tighter (for example, beyond
a given planning horizon for the present government) there may be
grounds for regarding additional financial supply as simply nonexistent
after a given date.

4.6 Intangible Effects

A particular kind of uncertainty concerns projects the effects of which
cannot be quantified or properly evaluated. This applies, for example,
to effects on human life and health, the natural environment and
aesthetic values. A large number of projects relevant for CB analysis
have important effects of this kind, for example, health services and
transportation projects.

We may distinguish three methods for approaching the problem of
estimating these so-called 'intangible' effects. It is often possible to estimate the order of magnitude of such effects or at least an upper or a
lower limit to their true size. This is sometimes achieved by an attempt
to translate the 'non-measurable' effects into measurable ones, which
the parties concerned regard as equivalent. For instance, damage to the
natural environment may in some cases be roughly estimated by the
additional costs (in time and money) for travelling to more distant and
untouched recreational areas. In other cases, it may be possible to establish a minimum value of an intangible effect. For example, a lower limit
to the value of a human life can be achieved by estimating a person's
contribution to net production. As is obvious from this example, the
minimum value that can be estimated may sometimes be far below the
'total value' of the effect.

In many cases approximations of, or minimum/maximum limits to,
the true value of project effects may be quite sufficient for reaching a
decision as to whether the project should be accepted or not. If not,
other approaches can be tried. One involves investigating how similar
effects have been taken into account in earlier decisions, by estimating
the upper or lower limit of the value that is revealed by earlier project
acceptances and refusals. For example, measures actually taken to avoid
traffic accidents would reveal an implicit (minimum) value of human
lives. Similarly, other measures of this nature, which have not been
taken because they were regarded as too expensive, would reveal a corresponding maximum value. To be specific, if investments in traffic security
in which costs per death avoided can be estimated to £100 000 have been
undertaken, whereas investments with estimated costs of £150 000 per
death accident have not, this could provide an interval for the implicit

value assigned to human life. However, repeated calculations of this type for a large number of different investment decisions where human lives are involved may present a quite inconsistent pattern and shatter the belief in the relevance of this approach. Such inconsistencies may be due to institutional inflexibilities or to a lack of perspective, which it is one of the aims of CB analysis (and so-called cost-effectiveness analysis) to help avoid.

If neither of these two approaches provides complete information about the total costs and benefits of a project, there remains a third approach. By combining all effects that it is meaningfully possible to combine into a single measure and by giving a separate account of those effects that cannot meaningfully be estimated in the same (money) terms, a multidimensional description of project outcome will be achieved and a decision will have to be reached on this basis. Although it might seem that CB analysis has failed in such cases, it should be observed that the decision problem has been simplified by the CB approach and by the consequent reduction of the original multidimensionality of the problem. Furthermore, it is now possible to conceive the order of magnitude of the intangible effects that would be implied by a yes or a no to the project proposal. For instance, if a project with negative intangibles and with positive net benefits of the other project effects were to be refuted, this would imply that the intangible effects were considered to be worth at least as much as these net benefits.

4.7   Applications of Cost–Benefit Analysis

CB analysis or elements of its techniques have been used in many areas of the public sector to evaluate, for example, defence projects, power plants, dam projects, irrigation, transportation projects such as bridges, roads, surface and underground rail services, health care, retraining of workers, education and research. As we pointed out in the introduction to this chapter, the field of application is much larger than examples of this kind reveal. In principle, all kinds of public decision-making can be guided or controlled by CB analysis.

For a selection of instructive case studies in which a CB analytic approach is used, the reader is referred to the list of suggested reading on page 148. The remainder of this chapter contains a brief outline of two applications of the approach. The first case probably represents one of the most important present and future fields of application: employment projects in chronically depressed areas. The second case is of a more specific nature: it concerns an attempt to estimate (or rather, identify) the effects of the introduction of commercial advertising on TV. This is a continuing issue in some countries in which there is a TV monopoly that is government-owned and financed by taxes. The purpose of this second application is to illustrate how the CB analysis approach can facilitate decision making in general, and not only decisions with respect to physical investment projects or projects all the effects of which can be assigned a defensible equivalent in money terms.

4.7.1   Cost–Benefit Analysis Applied to Investment Projects in Depressed Areas

The reason investment projects in depressed areas constitute an important field for applied CB analysis is that in most countries, it can be assumed that industry and service output in the future will expand rapidly in more densely populated areas, while small farms and small industry—in the absence of government support—will close down in more sparsely populated regions. The present structure of market prices may be responsible for an overly rapid development of this kind in the sense that market prices in urban areas may fall short of true social costs (for example, by neglecting congestion and other negative external effects of urban economic activity) and in the sense that market prices in rural areas exceed true social costs, in particular wages for labour otherwise unemployed. If this is the case and if the price structure were to be adjusted so as to reflect true social costs, more investment projects (and more employment opportunities) would be allocated to rural areas. Policy measures that alter regional investment allocation may thus be justified for reasons of social efficiency, that is to say, even without taking income distribution goals into account.

The outline of a CB analysis of an investment project in a depressed area is described in this section. We assume a known calculation of the expected profit of a supply-oriented project, which is typical for this kind of region, such as the opening-up of a new mine. The profitability calculation is assumed to show an expected loss, that is, the present value of expected money costs exceeds that of money revenue. On these grounds, private firms are unwilling to undertake the project. It now remains to be seen whether the social present value of the project is positive and, if so, whether the government in one way or another can and should see to it that the project is carried out[†].

---

† The case discussed in broad terms in this section refers to a CB study of a copper mine project in the north of Sweden.

(1) Recalculating a private present value to obtain a social present value: an example.   The main principles to be followed in computing a social present value (or CB value) for the project are (a) to modify the initial evaluations of project effects for which there is a difference in the private and social consequences and (b) to add such project effects, which were considered irrelevant when calculating the expected private present value.

(a) Modifying the evaluation of project effects
(i) We assume that the project would sell ore at an estimated world market price of £A per ton. The private present value (P) is based on this notation. If materialised, the mine would deliver ore to domestic buyers who would otherwise (we assume) have to import a corresponding quantity. Now, this may imply a smaller risk of a breakdown of ore deliveries to these buyers, allowing them to maintain smaller ore reserves. From the point of view of the economy as a whole, the benefits of the project should be revalued (by V_S) to take these reductions in storage costs into account.

(ii) The ore would be transported by rail from the mine to the buyers at costs that exceed the relevant marginal costs of transportation. (Railways rarely apply marginal cost pricing; moreover, in a case like this, the railway company may be in a monopoly position, which allows it to charge high transportation prices.) The costs of the project should therefore be reduced by the present value (V_T) of the difference between nominal transportation costs and the socially relevant transportation costs.

(iii) The mine company would employ labour at wages that are determined (we assume) by bargaining on a national level. If the mine project were the only available alternative in terms of providing new employment opportunities to unemployed people in the area, the persons affected might in fact have preferred to take jobs in the mine at, say, half the given wages rather than be without these opportunities and possibly be forced to leave the area. As it is extremely difficult to determine actual minimum acceptable wages for each individual (to be utilised as the relevant social labour costs in the CB calculation of the project), it will be necessary to make approximations along the following lines.

X per cent of those potentially employed in the project may be expected to have remained unemployed or underemployed in the same area during T_X years with an estimated production value of K_X and would then leave the area. Y per cent of the employees would otherwise be underemployed with a production value of K_y for T_y years and would then retire. The rest of the employees would otherwise have moved in the near future to an expanding region with higher production values but at a social cost, say, in the form of (government-financed) retraining and moving, including 'psychological costs' of moving, the latter 'intangible' being given a preliminary value for the time being. The present value of all these opportunity cost figures for the labour force affected by the project would fall short (by V_L) of the money wages as estimated in the private calculation. Hence, the private present value of the project should be adjusted upward by V_L to obtain the relevant social figure.

(iv) The private calculation may have been made at a rate of discount that deviates from what is considered to be relevant from the point of view of the economy as a whole. Recalculated at a 'proper' discount rate, the private present value of the project should be changed from P to P^*.

Given these four examples of modified project effects (on the benefit side by V_S, on the cost side by V_T and V_L and due to the change in discount rates) the present value of the project is changed from P to $P^* + V_S + V_T + V_L$. Projects effects that fall outside the mine company and thus have not been observed at all in the private profitability calculation now have to be added to this latter expression.

(b) Completing the set of project effects

(i) If carried out, the project would also indirectly give rise to increased employment in the region, for example, among sub-contractors to the mine company and among producers of consumer services. As private labour cos would exceed social labour costs in this instance also, these indirect employment effects also have to be taken into account. Assuming for simplicity that private production costs coincide approximately with prices for the goods and services concerned (see the discussion on page 94), the calculated benefit here would involve only the difference X_I between actual wage costs and labour opportunity costs as explained under (a) part (iii) above.

(ii) Since part of the population would have left the area sooner or later had the project not been carried out existing housing and capacity for social and commercial services would to some extent have been left idle. Simultaneously, the corresponding migration to areas with employment opportunities but no idle housing and service capacity would have required net investments in the housing and service sectors. Under these conditions, the project, if it materialised, would mean that real costs would be avoided (or postponed) to a present value of X_H.

(iii) The project may give rise to external effects of various kinds. Disposal of certain chemicals in a lake otherwise used for fishing and the increased wear and tear on roads due to heavy haulage to the railway sidings would lead to social costs equal to X_E.

After having specified and evaluated the additions to the set of project effects (as we have now indicated by way of a few examples), the preliminary social present value (net benefits) of the project may be calculated as

$$S = P^* + V_S + V_T + V_L + X_I + X_H - X_E$$

If an attempt were made to avoid overestimating benefit items and underestimating cost items, the resulting estimates of S could be interpreted as a lower bound to the true value of net benefits. Then, with $S > 0$, the project must be considered socially profitable. If S had been calculated the other way round to achieve an upper bound to the true value of net benefits, $S < 0$ must be interpreted to mean that the project is not worth while undertaking. Alternatively, sensitivity analysis could be carried out with respect to the most uncertain project effects, for example, with respect to 'psychological costs' mentioned under (a) part (iii) and (b) part (i). If S were to remain positive (negative) for variations over the interval for the uncertain items, the project could safely be regarded as socially profitable (unprofitable).

If the sign of S changes under a sensitivity analysis of this kind, the CB calculation loses its value as an unambiguous guide to the social profitability of the project. On the other hand, if the intervals relevant for sensitivity analysis are fairly small so that S remains close to zero under all circumstances, this would mean that it does not matter very much whether the project is undertaken or not.

(2) Should all projects with positive net benefits actually be carried out?   As we just stated, $S > 0$ means that the project can be regarded as socially profitable. More specifically, a positive S implies that there are positive net benefits, which in principle could be divided among all parties involved in such a way that nobody would be made worse off as a result of the project being undertaken; that is to say, the Pareto criterion could be met (see chapter 1). Now, we also know that the mine company in our example would actually have to pay wages accord-

ing to given agreements and not the (lower) social labour costs—and so on for other project items where social and private valuations differ. Hence, the project must be subsidised in order for the expected private profit (P) of the project to become positive. Unless the increased tax receipts from people directly or indirectly employed by the project turn out to be large enough, this means that taxpayers in general will have to pay for supplying underemployed persons in the depressed area with job opportunities. Thus, we would end up with a distribution of S by which the population in the depressed area receives all of the project net benefits (or more), while the rest of the population is made worse off. In other words, if this were the case, the Pareto criterion would not be met in practice.

Now, a division of project net benefits of the kind just described may, of course, be found acceptable or desirable on the basis of considerations of distribution policy. In fact, a majority of the group of taxpayers who are made worse off might even regard such redistributions as acceptable— particularly if they believed that future developments might very well affect them in a way similar to that experienced by people who live in depressed areas today. Thus, transfers to the underemployed may appear as a kind of insurance premium or 'guarantee' of future assistance in the event of unemployment.

Regardless of arguments of this kind, however, we know that governments have developed certain principles for assistance to regions with chronic employment problems. These principles may include the following forms of government support:

(a) Subsidies to projects in depressed areas amounting to £Z per person employed.

(b) General transfers to underemployed persons. These transfers may appear either as relief work, special transfers to local governments in depressed areas that make large welfare payments to the population, or direct and indirect transfers from the national government to low-income earners. The present value of these transfers can be calculated at £T per person.

(c) Government assistance to labour moving from depressed areas to regions with employment opportunities. The government may finance retraining of manpower, subsidise migration costs and/or make special transfers to local governments in localities where there is a large inflow of labour. The present value of these measures—intended to increase labour mobility—may be estimated at £M per person.

Given the existing principles for government transfers, we may estimate the reduction in total net transfers (equal to £Z, T or M per person)
that would result if the project under study were to be carried out.
Specifically, the project could be subsidised by at least (1) £Z per person
employed as a result of the project or (2) a combination of £T and £M
per person employed (net of changes in government tax receipts) depending on the extent to which people would have remained underemployed
in the region instead of moving to other regions [see point (a) part (iii)
in the previous section]. The reason that these amounts of subsidy are
regarded as acceptable is, of course, that according to stated principles
of distribution policy the government would have paid £Z per person
to projects increasing employment in depressed areas or a combination
of £T and £M if no such projects were available.

Summing up, if the government does not want to depart from existing principles of distribution policy, an investment project in depressed
areas should be accepted provided (a) the social present value of the
project is positive, that is, it is possible to achieve a change that could
satisfy the Pareto criterion, and (b) the subsidy required for the project
is less than the transfers that would otherwise be made. Given that both
conditions are fulfilled, the project can be carried out by either
government-owned firms or subsidised private firms.

4.7.2 A Cost–Benefit Approach to Analysing the Effects of the Introduction of Commercial Advertising on TV[†]

An attempt to answer the question of whether commercial advertising
should be allowed on TV may seem like an impossible task for objective
analysis. Personal values of an ethical or ideological nature might seem
to play an altogether decisive role. Nevertheless, we intend to demonstrate that it is possible to undertake an objective analysis, though incomplete, that would be sufficiently extensive to serve as an aid to
decision-making. In doing so, we shall be able to indicate how the CB
approach has a field of application that extends beyond physical investment projects of the type discussed in the preceding section.

Before addressing ourselves to the question itself, a basic observation
should be made. Contrary to popular belief, there are no economic
principles that make it necessary to introduce advertising as a means of

---

† This case-study can also be reversed without major modification to deal with
the effects of eliminating commercial advertising on TV. As it now stands, the
study draws on a more detailed report to a Swedish government committee investigating the general effects of the introduction of commercials on TV in Sweden.

financing the production of TV programmes. In fact, letting TV output depend on commercial advertising on TV is no more a logical necessity than it is to let, say, defence expenditures be determined by receipts from ads on military uniforms and vehicles. TV output will have to be determined in the same way as other public goods (see section 2.2), that is to say, primarily by an estimate of demand and production costs. And given that an increase in output is considered to be worth more than the relevant increase in production costs, the next step is to investigate which of the available financing methods (increased income taxes, sales taxes, licence fees, etc.) would be optimal. In other words, costs of TV broadcasting should be covered in the most efficient way, subject to constraints of distribution policy. (It may turn out, of course, that not even the best financing method is good enough to make a given increase in TV output worthwhile.)

Similarly, the introduction and extent of commercial advertising on TV will have to be determined, in the first place, by 'demand' and 'costs', that is by the social benefits and social costs of TV commercials. The ensuing financial surplus of this particular activity—if administered by the government—would reduce the need for other kinds of government revenue; in other words, reliance on the marginal, most unfavourable source of government revenue could be reduced. (Compare the preceding paragraph and the corresponding problem arising from an activity with a financial *deficit*.)

This section contains an attempt to analyse the problem: what are the social costs and benefits of the introduciton of commercials on TV?

(1) 'Direct' effects of TV commercials   (a) To begin with, let us assume that commercial advertising is purely informative, that is, that it informs potential consumers about the existence, properties, price, etc., of commodities. On this premise, the introduction of TV commercials has a beneficial social effect in that it makes the production of consumer information more efficient. The reason is, of course, that the resource use per person informed is much less than if other media are used. At the same time, it seems reasonable to assume that the main beneficial effect from the point of view of consumer information is limited to this cost reduction aspect; TV does not seem to make kinds of information available that cannot be obtained from media already in existence. (And this means that advertising on existing media will be reduced concomitantly with the introduction of TV commercials. We

may note that, already for this reason, it is inappropriate to treat the total revenues for TV commercials as an expression of the social benefits of increased consumer information; the reduced revenues for other media must be deducted.)

(b) Now we cannot, of course, accept the preceding assumption that commercial advertising is 'pure consumer information'. Without addressing ourselves to the difficult or even impossible question as to where to draw the line between informative and persuasive advertising, we can all agree that in the real world there are commercial messages of both kinds. In principle, persuasive messages can be regarded as 'negative' consumer information—such messages tend to make it harder for the consumer to determine what he really wants to buy. As TV is considered to be a medium of great power in influencing habits, attitudes, etc., of viewers, it seems necessary to take the risks of 'negative' consumer information into account.

The direct effect of the introduction of commercial advertising on TV may be summarised as follows. The introduction of TV commercials does not significantly affect the information basis for consumer decisions one way or the other, but the information provided will be produced at a lower cost.

(2) 'Indirect' effects of TV commercials   (a) The insertion of short commercials between or in the middle of programmes forces all viewers, regardless of whether or not they are interested, to watch the commercial messages or parts of them. Moreover, owing to the selection of pictures and sounds, all intended to make the viewer more observant, the commercials may be quite disturbing to the disinterested viewer. In addition to the adverse effects on this group of viewers, TV commercials may have adverse effects on all viewers' enjoyment of the interrupted or the following programme.

(b) Certain commercials, however, may be regarded as skillfully made, funny or interesting in other respects. Thus, among the viewers who do not find commercials disturbing, there may be quite a few who enjoy them as good entertainment.

(c) With the introduction of commercials on TV there will be a positive correlation between the popularity of programmes (the number of viewers) and advertising rates that can be charged. In this way, programme producers will be subjected to more or less direct pressure to make their programmes as popular as possible. With respect to programmes intended for 'general entertainment', this is or may be considered to be an important advantage. Programmes aimed at narrow viewer categories on the other hand, will run the risk of being eliminated altogether or at least being given only second-rate viewing time.

(3) Summarising direct and indirect effects   In the preceding section we indicated possible side effects or indirect effects of the introduction of commercial advertising on TV. All of these effects obviously belong to a group that hardly lends itself to measurement and evaluation. Although this may make it impossible to calculate a social present value as we did in the application in section 4.7.1, the CB approach may at least, as we have suggested, turn out to facilitate the decision process. An integration of all the effects mentioned above may take the following form, for example.

(I) The pros and cons of the guidance for programme design and scheduling mentioned under 2(c) may turn out to be such that no important net effect can be detected. Under such circumstances we may disregard this issue altogether.

(II) The fact that commercials may be considered to have an entertainment value (as we observed under 2(b)) can probably be offset by the introduction of additional entertainment programmes of the ordinary type to an extent equal to the time otherwise allotted to advertising. If so, point 2(b) would no longer play a decisive role.

(III) Points 1(a), 1(b) and 2(a) remain. They may be integrated by asking the question: is the potentially positive net effect of TV commercials from the resource use point of view large enough to outweigh the irritation that commercials cause among some groups of viewers?

For political decision-makers who accept the derivation of this final synthesised formulation of the issue and who find this formulation easier to grasp and respond to than that provided by 'traditional methods', the cost–benefit approach will have proved to be helpful.

Exercises to chapter 4.   Try to establish, along the schematic lines used in section 4.7, the main social cost and benefit items of the following projects:

(1) building a hydroelectric power station by an untouched river;
(2) constructing a new airport in a metropolitan region;
(3) introducing zero-fares in urban mass transit systems;
(4) vocational retraining of unemployed labour;
(5) raising water quality of a lake by reaeration.

4.8 Summary

In cost-benefit analysis an attempt is made to observe all effects of an investment project (or a policy alternative) that are of interest to the government with the ultimate purpose of ascertaining the net impact of the project on society and thus allowing conclusive comparisons with alternative projects or courses of action. When all the effects of a project cannot be identified or estimated, as is often the case, the ambition of CB analysis 'shrinks' from that of a decisive criterion to that of an instrument aimed at reducing the complexity of governmental decision making. The same is true, of course, if some policy objectives are not known to the analyst, or are not specified in sufficient detail.

Cost-benefit analysis, as commonly defined, is based on the assumption that social efficiency is one of the policy objectives. In that case positive net benefits mean that the project, in principle at least, could be designed so that no one would be made worse off by the introduction of the project. However, a specific version of the project—or perhaps even the only version feasible in practice—may not satisfy this (Pareto) criterion. In such cases the project cannot be accepted or rejected without the government's deciding whether it likes the *redistributive* consequences of the project or not.

Since we have assumed that one of the government's goals is social efficiency, cost-benefit analysis will incorporate most of the aspects discussed in the preceding parts of the book. In fact, it may be said that the use of CB analysis requires a firm grasp of the theory of social efficiency as presented earlier. Such demands make practical applications of the analysis fairly complex, of course, and often subject to theoretical problems in addition to the many, rather impressive, measurement problems already mentioned.

Mistakes in the practical application of cost-benefit analysis should certainly be criticised and often are. Unfortunately, such criticism is sometimes interpreted to mean that even the principles of the general approach of cost-benefit analysis are invalid. This is incorrect, however, as long as the government is concerned with efficiency.

APPENDIX 1. NECESSARY CONDITIONS FOR PARETO OPTIMALITY

A1-1   A Derivation of the Necessary Conditions for Pareto Optimality in a 'Perfect' Economy

This appendix contains a more rigorous presentation of the necessary conditions for Pareto-optimal allocation of resources than was given in the text. As in chapter 1, we deal with an economy with only two commodities (1 and 2) and two consumers both of whom are assumed to consume some of each of the two commodities. We assume, moreover, that there are two factors of production (L and K). One of them may be supplied in variable quantities by the consumers (labour, L) and the other refers to a resource available in a given quantity (say, machines or real capital, K).

A1.1.1   Let us first introduce the following assumptions with respect to the consumers in the economy.

(1)   The individual consumer (i) is only interested in his own consumption of commodities (x_{i1}, x_{i2}) and his own supply of factor L (L_i).

(2)   The consumer is able to rank, in a consistent or *transitive* order of preference, all possibly interesting combinations of x_{i1}, x_{i2} and L_i. This means for three different such combinations C_1, C_2 and C_3, that if $C_1 >$ (is preferred to) C_2 and $C_2 > C_3$, then $C_1 > C_3$. Similarly, if i is indifferent ($\sim$) to C_1 and C_2, that is, $C_1 \sim C_2$, and $C_2 \sim C_3$, then $C_1 \sim C_3$. (This assumption may be called a *rationality* assumption.)

(3)   There is, in the neighbourhood of each combination C_1 another combination C_2, which contains more of one commodity and less of the other, such that the consumer is indifferent to the two combinations (so-called *continuous preferences*).

The assumptions of transitive and continuous preferences, (2) and (3), combined with a few purely formal assumptions of no economic significance, imply that the ranking assumed in (2) can be described by a continuous *function*, a so-called preference function or utility function $u^i(x_{i1}, x_{i2}, L_i)$ such that

$$u^i(\bar{x}_{i1}, \bar{x}_{i2}, \bar{L}_i) > u^i(\bar{\bar{x}}_{i1}, \bar{\bar{x}}_{i2}, \bar{\bar{L}}_i) \text{ if } \bar{C} > \bar{\bar{C}}$$
$$u^i(\bar{x}_{i1}, \bar{x}_{i2}, \bar{L}_i) = u^i(\bar{\bar{x}}_{i1}, \bar{\bar{x}}_{i2}, \bar{\bar{L}}_i) \text{ if } \bar{C} \sim \bar{\bar{C}}$$
$$u^i(\bar{x}_{i1}, \bar{x}_{i2}, \bar{L}_i) < u^i(\bar{\bar{x}}_{i1}, \bar{\bar{x}}_{i2}, \bar{\bar{L}}_i) \text{ if } \bar{C} < \bar{\bar{C}}$$

where $\bar{C}$ and $\bar{\bar{C}}$ stand for the combinations $(\bar{x}_{i1}, \bar{x}_{i2}, \bar{L}_i)$ and $(\bar{\bar{x}}_{i1}, \bar{\bar{x}}_{i2}, \bar{\bar{L}}_i)$, respectively. The function $u^i(\quad)$ is a so-called *ordinal* preference function; that is, it describes a ranking only and does not say anything about how much better or more preferable one combination is than another. In addition, it should be observed that assuming the existence of an ordinal preference function does not amount to anything other than making assumptions (2) and (3). That is to say, whenever assumptions (2) and (3) are made, we may equally well use an ordinal preference function.

A1.1.2 Before proceeding to a description of the producer side of the economy, let us point out that, in a barter economy where given amounts of the two commodities, $\bar{x}_1$ and $\bar{x}_2$, are to be distributed among the consumers and where we disregard how these quantities are produced (and thus abstract from L and K), the necessary conditions for a Pareto optimal consumption distribution can be derived in the following manner.

Maximise $u^A(x_{A1}, x_{A2})$ given the constraint that consumer B is not to be made worse off, $u^B(x_{B1}, x_{B2}) = \bar{u}^B$. This constrained maximisation problem can be formulated as the maximisation of the following function

$$u^A(x_{A1}, x_{A2}) + \lambda[u^B(\bar{x}_1 - x_{A1}, \bar{x}_2 - x_{A2}) - \bar{u}^B]$$

a so-called Lagrange function where λ is an unknown so-called Lagrange multiplier. Differentiating this function with respect to the variables x_{A1} and x_{A2} and setting these partial derivatives equal to zero, we obtain the following necessary conditions for optimum (here: maximum).

$$\frac{\partial u^A}{\partial x_{A1}} - \lambda \frac{\partial u^B}{\partial x_{B1}} = 0^\dagger$$

and

$$\frac{\partial u^A}{\partial x_{A2}} - \lambda \frac{\partial u^B}{\partial x_{B1}} = 0$$

or, after eliminating λ

$$\left(\frac{\partial u^A}{\partial x_{A1}}\right)\bigg/\left(\frac{\partial u^A}{\partial x_{A2}}\right) = \left(\frac{\partial u^B}{\partial x_{B1}}\right)\bigg/\left(\frac{\partial u^B}{\partial x_{B2}}\right)$$

With a different system of notation, the last expression can be rewritten as

$$MRS^A_{21} = MRS^B_{21}\ddagger$$

This is the condition for Pareto optimality in a barter economy, familiar from chapter 1 (see also the diagrammatical exposition in figure 1.2).

A1.1.3 Turning to an economy with production, we assume that two companies (I and II) produce commodity 1 in accordance with the following production functions

$$q^I_1 = q^I_1(L^I, K^I)$$
$$q^{II}_1 = q^{II}_1(L^{II}, K^{II})$$

Each of these functions is assumed to reflect efficiency in the sense that it is technically impossible for the firm to achieve a larger output with given inputs, or, the same output with less inputs, than is indicated by the function.

---

† The second term on the left-hand side is obtained in the following way

$$\lambda \frac{\partial u^B}{\partial x_B}, \times \frac{\partial x_{B1}}{\partial x_{A1}} = \lambda \frac{\partial u^B}{\partial x_{B1}} \times \frac{\partial(\bar{x}_1 - x_{A1})}{\partial x_{A1}} = \lambda \frac{\partial u^B}{\partial x_{B1}}(-1) = -\lambda \frac{\partial u^B}{\partial x_{B1}}$$

‡ For shifts along an *indifference curve*

$$du^A = \frac{\partial u^A}{\partial x_{A1}} dx_{A1} + \frac{\partial u^A}{\partial x_{A2}} dx_{A2} = 0$$

This means that the marginal rate of substitution

$$MRS^A_{21} \equiv -\frac{dx_{A2}}{dx_{A1}} = \left(\frac{\partial u^A}{\partial x_{A1}}\right)\bigg/\left(\frac{\partial u^A}{\partial x_{A2}}\right)$$

Efficient production in the industry for commodity 1 is obtained when given quantities of the factors of production, say, $\bar{L}$ and $\bar{K}$, are allocated to the firms so that $q_1 = q_1^I + q_1^{II}$ attains a maximum. The necessary conditions for a maximum of $q_1 = q_1^I(L^I, K^I) + q_1^{II}(\bar{L} - L^I, \bar{K} - K^I)$ can be derived as

$$\frac{\partial q_1^I}{\partial L^I} - \frac{\partial q_1^{II}}{\partial L^{II}} = 0$$

$$\frac{\partial q_1^I}{\partial K^I} - \frac{\partial q_1^{II}}{\partial K^{II}} = 0$$

or

$$\frac{\partial q_1^I}{\partial L^I} = \frac{\partial q_1^{II}}{\partial L^{II}} \qquad \text{and} \qquad \frac{\partial q_1^I}{\partial K^I} = \frac{\partial q_1^{II}}{\partial K^{II}}$$

that is

$$MP_{1L}^I = MP_{1L}^{II} \qquad \text{and} \qquad MP_{1K}^I = MP_{1K}^{II}$$

Corresponding expressions can be derived in the same manner for companies III and IV in the industry producing commodity 2.

The necessary conditions for efficient production in the economy as a whole are obtained as follows. Assume that we have an efficient allocation of resources among companies *within* each industry, that is that the conditions just mentioned are met. This means that each allocation of L and K among industries will give rise to a particular volume of output of the two commodities.

The total output in the economy is efficient if q_1 is maximised, given a certain quantity of commodity 2, $\bar{q}_2$. Efficient production with given resources $\bar{L}$ and $\bar{K}$, where $\bar{L} = L^1 + L^2$ and $\bar{K} = K^1 + K^2$, can thus be obtained by maximising

$$q_1 = q_1(L^1, K^1) \qquad \text{or} \qquad q_2 = q_2(L^2, K^2)$$

The necessary conditions here are

$$\frac{\partial q_1}{\partial L^1} - \lambda \frac{\partial q_2}{\partial L^2} = 0$$

and

$$\frac{\partial q_1}{\partial K^1} - \lambda \frac{\partial q_2}{\partial K^2} = 0$$

Eliminating the Lagrange multiplier λ, these conditions may be formulated as

$$\left(\frac{\partial q_1}{\partial L^1}\right)\bigg/\left(\frac{\partial q_1}{\partial K^1}\right) = \left(\frac{\partial q_2}{\partial L^2}\right)\bigg/\left(\frac{\partial q_2}{\partial K^2}\right) \quad \text{or} \quad \left(\frac{\partial q_1}{\partial L^1}\right)\bigg/\left(\frac{\partial q_2}{\partial L^2}\right) = \left(\frac{\partial q_1}{\partial K^1}\right)\bigg/\left(\frac{\partial q_2}{\partial K^2}\right)$$

that is

$$\mathrm{MRT}^1_{KL} = \mathrm{MRT}^2_{KL} \qquad \text{or} \qquad \mathrm{MRT}^L_{21} = \mathrm{MRT}^K_{21}$$

(also called the 'marginal rate of factor substitution' of K for L with respect to commodities 1 and 2, respectively)

(also called the 'marginal rate of product transformation' of commodity 1 into commodity 2 concerning factors L and K, respectively)

Our assumptions imply that

$$\frac{\partial q_1^{\mathrm{I}}}{\partial L^{\mathrm{I}}} = \frac{\partial q_1^{\mathrm{II}}}{\partial L^{\mathrm{II}}}$$

and thus

$$\frac{\partial q_1^{\mathrm{I}}}{\partial L^{\mathrm{I}}} = \frac{\partial q_1^{\mathrm{II}}}{\partial L^{\mathrm{II}}} = \frac{\partial q_1}{\partial L^1}$$

and so on for all other partial derivatives in the set of optimum conditions just derived. This means that in a Pareto optimum the marginal rates of transformation must be identical for all companies in the economy, that is, that

$$\mathrm{MRT}^{\mathrm{I}}_{KL} = \mathrm{MRT}^{\mathrm{II}}_{KL} \ (= \mathrm{MRT}^1_{KL} = \mathrm{MRT}^2_{KL}) = \mathrm{MRT}^{\mathrm{III}}_{KL} = \mathrm{MRT}^{\mathrm{IV}}_{KL}$$

and

$$\mathrm{MRT}^L_{\mathrm{III\ I}} = \mathrm{MRT}^L_{\mathrm{IV\ I}} = \cdots = \mathrm{MRT}^L_{\mathrm{IV\ II}} = \mathrm{MRT}^K_{\mathrm{III\ I}} = \cdots = \mathrm{MRT}^K_{\mathrm{IV\ II}}$$

(see chapter 1).

A1.1.4 After these derivations of some of the necessary conditions for Pareto optimality in partial contexts we may now proceed directly to a derivation of the complete set of necessary conditions for efficient allocation in the economy as a whole. This allocation problem may be described as the maximisation of u^{A}, given that:

(1) $u^{\mathrm{B}} = \bar{u}^{\mathrm{B}}$;

(2) there is efficient production within companies, that is, that the individual production functions are assumed to hold;

(3) production (or supply) equals demand for each commodity and each factor.

In other words, the problem amounts to maximising the following expression

$$u^A(x_{A1}, x_{A2}, L_A) +$$
$$\lambda[u^B(x_{B1}, x_{B2}, L_B) - \bar{u}^B] +$$
$$\mu_1[q_1^I(L^I, K^I) + q_1^{II}(L^{II}, K^{II}) - x_{A1} - x_{B1}] + \qquad \text{(commodity 1)}$$
$$\mu_2[q_2^{III}(L^{III}, K^{III}) + q_2^{IV}(L^{IV}, K^{IV}) - x_{A2} - x_{A2}] + \qquad \text{(commodity 2)}$$

$$\rho_1\left[L_A + L_B - \sum_I^{IV} L^j\right] + \qquad\qquad\qquad\qquad \text{(factor } L)$$

$$\rho_k\left[\bar{K} - \sum_I^{IV} K^j\right] \qquad\qquad\qquad\qquad\qquad \text{(factor } K)$$

Differentiating this function with respect to all variables ($x_{A1}, x_{B1}, x_{A2}, x_{B2}, L_A, L_B$ for the consumers and L^j, K^j for the four producers, j = I, II, III and IV) we obtain the necessary conditions for Pareto optimality in the economy as a whole. These conditions are presented in table 1. Rearranging the conditions as they initially appear in column 2 to eliminate the Lagrange multipliers (λ, ρ_i and μ_i), we arrive at the formulation in terms of marginal rates of substitution and transformation (see columns 3 and 5) familiar from chapter 1. (The numbers in column 4 refer to the Pareto-optimality conditions as denoted in chapter 1.)

A1.1.5 We have derived the necessary conditions for Pareto optimality in an economy independent of whether it is a market economy or a centrally planned, non-market economy. Our objective now is to demonstrate that these conditions are automatically fulfilled in a particular type of market economy. As we shall see, the Lagrange multipliers μ_1, μ_2, ρ_1 and ρ_2 can be interpreted in this context as market prices according to which consumers and producers adjust their economic behaviour.

Let us test the proposition just made by regarding μ_1 and μ_2 as prices for commodities 1 and 2, and ρ_1 and ρ_2 as prices for (the services from) factors L and K. For a consumer (say, consumer A) who is maximising his preference function (see pages 128–9)

$$u^A(x_{A1}, x_{A2}, L_A)$$

subject to the budget constraint, $\mu_1 x_{A1} + \mu_2 x_{A2} - \rho_1 L_A = 0$

TABLE 1: NECESSARY CONDITIONS FOR PARETO OPTIMALITY

Column	1 Derivative with respect to	2 Necessary conditions		3 Compilation of conditions
Consumption	x_{i1}	$\dfrac{\partial u^A}{\partial x_{A1}} - \mu_1 = 0;$	$\lambda \dfrac{\partial u^B}{\partial x_{B1}} - \mu_1 = 0$	$\dfrac{\dfrac{\partial u^A}{\partial x_{A1}}}{\dfrac{\partial u^A}{\partial x_{A2}}} = \dfrac{\dfrac{\partial u^B}{\partial x_{B1}}}{\dfrac{\partial u^B}{\partial x_{B2}}} = \dfrac{\mu_1}{\mu_2}$
	x_{i2}	$\dfrac{\partial u^A}{\partial x_{A2}} - \mu_2 = 0;$	$\lambda \dfrac{\partial u^B}{\partial x_{B2}} - \mu_2 = 0$	
	L_j	$\dfrac{\partial u^A}{\partial L_A} + \rho_1 = 0;$	$\lambda \dfrac{\partial u^B}{\partial L_B} + \rho_1 = 0 \rightarrow$	corresp.

$$L^j \begin{cases} \mu_1 \dfrac{\partial q_1^{I}}{\partial L^{I}} - \rho_1 = 0; & \mu_1 \dfrac{\partial q_1^{II}}{\partial L^{II}} - \rho_1 = 0 \rightarrow & \dfrac{\partial q_1^{I}}{\partial L^{I}} = \dfrac{\partial q_1^{II}}{\partial L^{II}} = \dfrac{\rho_1}{\mu_1} \\[3ex] \mu_2 \dfrac{\partial q_2^{III}}{\partial L^{III}} - \rho_1 = 0; & \mu_2 \dfrac{\partial q_2^{IV}}{\partial L^{IV}} - \rho_1 = 0 \rightarrow & \text{corresp.} \end{cases}$$

$$K^j \begin{cases} \mu_1 \dfrac{\partial q_1^{I}}{\partial K^{I}} - \rho_2 = 0; & \text{corresp.} \rightarrow & \text{corresp.} \\[3ex] \mu_2 \dfrac{\partial q_2^{III}}{\partial K^{III}} - \rho_2 = 0; & \text{corresp.} \rightarrow & \text{corresp.} \end{cases}$$

Production

$$\begin{cases} \dfrac{\dfrac{\partial q_1^{I}}{\partial L^{I}}}{\dfrac{\partial q_1^{I}}{\partial K^{I}}} = \dfrac{\dfrac{\partial q_2^{III}}{\partial L^{III}}}{\dfrac{\partial q_2^{III}}{\partial K^{III}}} = \dfrac{\rho_1}{\rho_2} \\[5ex] \dfrac{\dfrac{\partial q_2^{III}}{\partial L^{III}}}{\dfrac{\partial q_1^{I}}{\partial L^{I}}} = \dfrac{\dfrac{\partial q_2^{III}}{\partial K^{III}}}{\dfrac{\partial q_1^{I}}{\partial K^{I}}} = \dfrac{\mu_1}{\mu_2} \end{cases}$$

corresp.

Consumption and production	In addition, it follows from the above conditions (see the Lagrange multipliers in column 5) that
	and that
	If the consumers supply two kinds of factors, P_1 and P_2, then
	and

4	5

Interpretation

$\rightarrow$ (1) $MRS_{21}^A = MRS_{21}^B$ $\left(= \dfrac{\mu_1}{\mu_2} \right)$ Consumers' marginal rates of substitution for each pair of commodities must be the same.

$\rightarrow$ (2) $MRS_{L1}^A = MRS_{L1}^B$ $\left(= \dfrac{\mu_1}{\rho_1} \right)$ Consumers' marginal rates of substitution between a commodity, say, commodity 1, and a factor supplied by the consumers must be the same.

$\rightarrow$ (3) $MP_{1L}^I = MP_{1L}^{II}$ $\left(= \dfrac{\rho_1}{\mu_1} \right)$ The marginal rates of transformation between a factor and a commodity—

$\rightarrow$ (3) $MP_{2L}^{III} = MP_{2L}^{IV}$ $\left(= \dfrac{\rho_1}{\mu_2} \right)$ that is, the marginal product of the factor—must be identical for all producers of the commodity in question.

$\rightarrow$ corresp.

$\rightarrow$ corresp.   Ditto (with reference to factor K).

$\rightarrow$ (5) $MRT_{KL}^I = MRT_{KL}^{III}$ $\left(= \dfrac{\rho_1}{\rho_2} \right)$ The marginal rates of transformation for each pair of factors—or, if we like, the marginal rates of factor substitution—must be identical for all producers.

$\rightarrow$ (9) $MRT_{21}^L = MRT_{21}^K$ $\left(= \dfrac{\mu_1}{\mu_2} \right)$ The marginal rates of transformation for each pair of commodities must be the same for all factors.

$\rightarrow$ corresp.

(8) $MRS_{21}^i = MRT_{21}^L$ $\left(= \dfrac{\mu_1}{\mu_2} \right)$ Marginal rates of substitution (for all consumers) and transformation (for all producers) must be identical for each commodity pair,
     etc.

(9) $MRS_{1L}^i = MP_{1L}^i$ $\left(= \dfrac{\rho_1}{\mu_1} \right)$ each commodity–factor pair, and also
     etc.

[(6) $MRS_{P_1 P_2}^A = MRS_{P_2 P_1}^B$]

(7) $MRS_{P_1 P_2}^i = MRT_{P_1 P_2}^i$ for each factor pair.

where μ_1, μ_2 and ρ_1 are regarded as given market prices, that is, a consumer maximising the Lagrange function

$$u^A(x_{A1}, x_{A2}, L_A) - \gamma(\mu_1 x_{A1} + \mu_2 x_{A2} - \rho_1 L_A)$$

we obtain the following necessary conditions for maximum

$$\frac{\partial u^A}{\partial x_{A1}} - \gamma\mu_1 = 0; \qquad \frac{\partial u^A}{\partial x_{A2}} - \gamma\mu_2 = 0; \qquad \frac{\partial u^A}{\partial L_A} + \gamma\rho_1 = 0$$

$$MRS_{21}^A = \frac{\mu_1}{\mu_2}; \qquad MRS_{1L}^A = \frac{\rho_1}{\mu_1}$$

In other words, if μ_1, μ_2 and ρ_1 are market determined prices and if all consumers behave (roughly) in the way just indicated, conditions (1) and (2), necessary for reaching a Pareto optimum in the economy, will be fulfilled (see column 4 in table 1).

Moreover, if a producer (say, producer I of commodity 1) maximises his profits

$$\mu_1 q_1^I(L^I, K^I) - \rho_1 L^I - \rho_2 K^I$$

he will meet the necessary conditions for maximum

$$\mu_1 \frac{\partial q_1^I}{\partial L^I} - \rho_1 = 0; \qquad \mu_1 \frac{\partial q_1^I}{\partial K^I} - \rho_2 = 0$$

and hence

$$MP_{1L}^I = \frac{\rho_1}{\mu_1}; \qquad MRT_{KL}^I = \frac{\rho_1}{\rho_2}$$

In other words, if μ_1, μ_2, ρ_1 and ρ_2 are market-determined prices and if all producers behave (roughly) as profit maximisers, conditions (3) and (5) necessary for Pareto optimality are met.

Checking this procedure for all conditions (1) to (9) in table 1, we should find that 'profit and utility maximising' behaviour in the presence of market-determined prices implies that all necessary conditions for Pareto optimality are fulfilled in the economy specified here. We should also find that this conclusion is not affected by increasing the number of consumers, producers, commodities and factors to realistic levels. Nor would the conclusion be affected if we extended the model to describe an intertemporal or multiperiod economy where there was certainty about future prices.

Finally, we should note that the fulfilment of the Pareto optimum conditions in a market economy requires an equality between marginal costs (MC) and the corresponding market prices (except for uninteresting special cases). This can be demonstrated in the following way. The total costs (C) for producer I are defined as

$$C \equiv \rho_1 L^I + \rho_2 K^I$$

where ρ_1 and ρ_2 are market prices for using the two factors, respectively. In addition, we have the production function

$$q_1^I = q_1^I(L^I, K^I)$$

Now, differentiating the cost and production functions for producer I, we obtain

$$dC = \rho_1 dL^I + \rho_2 dK^I$$

$$dq_1^I = \frac{\partial q_1^I}{\partial L^I} dL^I + \frac{\partial q_1^I}{\partial K^I} dK^I$$

Dividing the first expression by the second and postulating that the following conditions necessary for Pareto optimality are fulfilled

$$(MP_{1L}^I =) \frac{\partial q_1^I}{\partial L^I} = \frac{\rho_1}{\mu_1} \quad \text{and} \quad (MP_{1K}^I =) \frac{\partial q_1^I}{\partial K^I} = \frac{\rho_2}{\mu_1}$$

then

$$MC \equiv \frac{dC}{dq_1^I} = \frac{\rho_1 dL^I + \rho_2 dK^I}{(\partial q_1^I/\partial L^I)dL^I + (\partial q_1^I/\partial K^I)dK^I} =$$

$$= \frac{\rho_1 dL^I + \rho_2 dK^I}{1/\mu_1(\rho_1 dL^I + \rho_2 dK^I)} = \mu_1$$

Thus, it follows from the fact that the Pareto optimum conditions are met that $MC = \mu_1$. Similarly, it can be shown that a Pareto optimum in a market economy requires that marginal costs equal prices for all other commodities as well. (This result may be given the following alternative formulation: What the consumers must give up (in terms of other commodities) to obtain an additional unit of a certain commodity (a sacrifice that is reflected by marginal costs in a perfect market economy) corresponds in optimum to the amount of other goods that the consumers are willing to give up, an amount which, in a perfect market economy, is reflected by the market price of the commodity in question.)

A1.2 Optimum Conditions in the Presence of Imperfections

The necessary conditions for Pareto optimality derived in the preceding section referred to a 'perfect' economy, that is, an economy with only private goods, no decreasing-cost industries and no external effects. Moreover, with respect to the perfect market economy dealt with in the final part of the preceding section, we assumed that there is perfect competition (market-determined prices) as well as equilibrium on all markets. We now turn to a demonstration of how the optimum conditions must be modified in the presence of technical as well as behavioural imperfections.

A1.2.1 External effects in production exist if, for example, the output of producer II affects the production of producer I, thus changing the production function of producer I (see page 130) to

$$q_1^I = q_1^I(L^I, K^I, q^{II})$$

where $\partial q_1^I / \partial q_1^{II} \neq 0$. In order to find the optimum conditions for an economy with external effects of this kind, the Lagrange function on page 133 has to be modified with respect to the production function concerned. By differentiating the revised Langrange function with respect to L^{II} and thus determining the total effect of changes in L^{II} on the economy, the earlier condition, $\mu_1(\partial q_1^{II}/\partial L^{II}) = \rho_1$, can be replaced by the new one

$$\mu_1 \frac{\partial q_1^{II}}{\partial L^{II}} + \mu_1 \frac{\partial q_1^I}{\partial q_1^{II}} \frac{\partial q_1^{II}}{\partial L^{II}} = \rho_1$$

This condition may be slightly rearranged as

$$\frac{\partial q_1^{II}}{\partial L^{II}} \left(1 + \frac{\partial q_1^I}{\partial q_1^{II}} \right) = \frac{\rho_1}{\mu_1} \tag{2.1.1}$$

which can be compared with the corresponding expression in column 3, table 1. The left-hand side, showing the marginal product for the economy as a whole of employing factor L in company II, now deviates from the return accruing to company II, $\partial q_1^{II}/\partial L^{II}$, due to the existence of an external effect.

The new optimum condition (2.1.1) and a corresponding condition for factor K^{II} are not met if company II behaves as a profit maximiser.

As we saw in the preceding section, profit-maximising behaviour would
lead to

$$\frac{\partial q_1^{II}}{\partial L^{II}} = \frac{\rho_1}{\mu_1}$$

where μ_1 and ρ_1 again are interpreted as market prices. However, if the
price received by firm II for commodity 1 were adjusted by government
intervention so that firm II instead faced the following price ratio

$$\frac{\rho_1}{\mu_1 \, (1 + \partial q_1^I / \partial q_1^{II})}$$

profit-maximising behaviour would imply fulfilling the condition for
Pareto optimality. This element of economic policy amounts to levying
a tax of $\mu_1(\partial q_1^I/\partial q_1^{II})$ per unit of commodity 1 on the output of company
II whenever $\partial q_1^{II}/\partial q_1^{II} < 0$, that is, whenever the external effect is negative,
and to introducing a corresponding subsidy in the presence of a positive
external effect.

Similar alterations in the optimum conditions would result from the
appearance of external effects elsewhere in the economy, for example,
in consumption activities as well.

A1.2.2   If there exists a public good, called commodity 3, so defined
that all individuals consume the same amount of the commodity, that is
$x_{A3} = x_{B3} = q_3$, the optimum problem from page 133 will be affected
in three ways:

(1) The preference functions will now be

$$u^i(x_{i1}, x_{i2}, L_i, q_3)$$

(2) The production of the public good is taken care of by a (publicly
owned and/or a publicly administered) company V having the production
function $q_3 = q_3^V(L^V, K^V)$. Hence, there is an additional constraint to
the optimum problem

$$\mu_3 [q_3^V(L^V, K^V) - q_3]$$

(3) Adding a fifth company causes the expressions for equilibrium
in the factor markets to change. Thus the corresponding constraints of
the optimum problem will be

$$\rho_1 \left[L_A + L_B - \sum_I^V L^j \right]$$

and

$$\rho_2\left[\bar{K} - \overset{V}{\underset{I}{\Sigma}}K^j\right]$$

Now, differentiating the Lagrange function with respect to the new variable q_3 also, we obtain the additional optimum condition

$$\frac{\partial u^A}{\partial q_3} + \lambda\frac{\partial u^B}{\partial q_3} - \mu_3 = 0$$

which after dividing by μ_1 and eliminating μ_1 and μ_1/λ using the other optimum conditions, $\mu_1 = \partial u^A/\partial u_{A1}$ and $\mu_1/\lambda = \partial u^B/\partial x_{B1}$ (compare row 1, column 1 in table 1), can be written as

$$\frac{(\partial u^A/\partial q_3)}{(\partial u^A/\partial x_{A1})} + \frac{(\partial u^B/\partial q_3)}{(\partial u^B/\partial x_{B1})} = \frac{\mu_3}{\mu_1} \qquad \text{or} \qquad \overset{B}{\underset{i=A}{\Sigma}} \text{MRS}^i_{13} = \frac{\mu_3}{\mu_1}$$

Furthermore, differentiating with respect to L^V and K^V, we obtain

$$\mu_3\frac{\partial q_3^V}{\partial L^V} - \rho_1 = 0; \qquad \mu_3\frac{\partial q_3^V}{\partial K^V} - \rho_2 = 0$$

which combined with two of the other optimum conditions, $\mu_1(\partial q_1^I/\partial L^I) - \rho_1 = 0$ and $\mu_1(\partial q_1^I/\partial K^I) = \rho_2$, becomes

$$\frac{(\partial q_1^I/\partial L^I)}{(\partial q_3^V/\partial L^V)} = \frac{(\partial q_1^I/\partial K^I)}{(\partial q_3^V/\partial K^V)} = \frac{\mu_3}{\mu_1}$$

or

$$\text{MRT}^L_{13} = \text{MRT}^K_{13} = \frac{\mu_3}{\mu_1}$$

Thus, it follows that $\Sigma\,\text{MRS}^i_{13} = \text{MRT}^L_{13} = \cdots$, that is, that in optimum the sum of the individual marginal rates of substitution between a public commodity and a private commodity must equal the corresponding marginal rates of transformation.

A1.2.3 Decreasing Average Costs

Introducing an additional private commodity, commodity 4, let us first of all define the position in which all the optimum conditions of the kind described thus far are fulfilled. In this position, the variables are assumed to take on values indicated by an asterisk (*): $x^*_{A1}, x^*_{B1}, \cdots$

x_{A4}^*, x_{B4}^*, etc. As before, all variables are assumed to be strictly positive (> 0). Now, if commodity 4—in contrast to the other commodities—
is produced at decreasing average costs, it may turn out that $x_{A4} + x_{B4} = 0$
is to be preferred to $x_4^* = x_{A4}^* + x_{B4}^*$ (> 0). The answer to the question
about the optimum volume of output, x_4^* or 0, is obtained by comparing
$u^A(x_{A1}^*, x_{B2}^*, L_A^*, x_{A4}^*)$ and the maximum of $u^A(x_{A1}, x_{A2}, L_A, 0) +$
$\lambda[u^B(x_{B1}, x_{B2}, L_B, 0) - \bar{u}^B] + \cdots$, where the latter maximum is that
derived in section A1.1.4, that is, prior to observing the possible existence
of commodity 4. Denoting the values of the variables in the latter (local)
maximum by**, we thus have to find out whether

$$u^A(x_{A1}^*, x_{A2}^*, L_A^*, x_{A4}^*) > u^A(x_{A1}^{**}, x_{A2}^{**}, L_A^{**}, 0)$$

in order for x_4^* to be Pareto optimal.

This is a brief description of the investment criterion mentioned in
chapter 2 and of the additional condition (a so-called 'total condition')
that must be fulfilled over and above the 'marginal conditions' (that is,
the previously derived optimum conditions), for the existence of a
decreasing-cost industry to be compatible with social efficiency.

A1.2.4   Disequilibrium

Let us now leave the 'technical imperfections' (that is, deviations from
the assumptions about the type of commodities, production functions
and preference functions in the perfect economy) to observe the consequences of a behavioural 'imperfection' in a market economy.

All assumptions are again as in section A1.1.4. Here, however, we deal
explicitly with a market economy in which prices p_1 and p_2 have been
established for commodities 1 and 2, respectively. Now, at this particular
set of prices, the market for commodity 1 is characterised by a situation
of disequilibrium, say, by a state of excess demand. This means that one
or both of consumers A and B fail to reach their individual optimum
positions at the given prices. The situation for a consumer whose market
demand is not satisfied is described in figure A1, where $\bar{x}_{i1}$ is the maximum attainable volume of commodity 1 for consumer i and where
$x_{i1}^{opt.}$ is the desired volume at the given income and prices. Thus, for at
least one consumer i

$$\text{MRS}_{21}^i \neq \frac{p_1}{p_2} \qquad \text{(see point P in the figure)}$$

Furthermore, as we assume that the remaining optimum conditions are
fulfilled and that the producers behave such that $\text{MRT}_{21}^j = p_1/p_2$, then

$MRS^i_{21} \neq MRT^i_{21}$ for at least one i. Thus, we can see that a situation of disequilibrium such as this makes it impossible for the market economy to reach a Pareto optimum position.

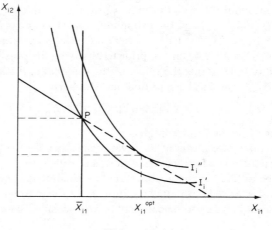

Figure A1.1

A1.2.5 Imperfect Competition

Assume now that behaviour in a market economy is imperfect in the sense that a company VI producing commodity 4 acts as a profit-maximising monopolist. As usual, a profit maximum is attained at the price and volume of output where marginal costs (MC) equal marginal revenue (MR). Now, as $p_4 >$ MR for a firm in a monopoly situation, in contrast to the equality of prices and marginal revenues under perfect competition, $p_4 >$ MC at the profit maximum level. As we have seen, however, a Pareto optimum in an otherwise perfect market economy requires that prices equal marginal costs. More specifically, it follows from the presentation in section A1.1.5 that the Pareto optimum condition, $MP^{VI}_{1j} = p_j/p_1$, where p_j is the price for using a unit of factor j $(j = L, K)$, cannot be fulfilled in the presence of imperfectly competitive behaviour.

APPENDIX 2. THE CONSUMER'S SURPLUS

In order to obtain a step-by-step derivation of the consumer's surplus, we begin with a situation in which a certain commodity (commodity 1) is assumed to be the only commodity produced and marketed in the economy. Given the commodity price and the consumer's income, the consumer is then able to reach point A in figure A2.1. Now, assume

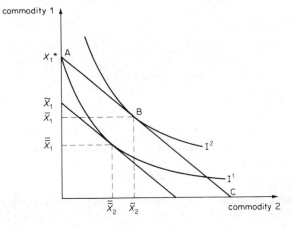

Figure A2.1

that a new product (commodity 2) is introduced and made available at a price equal to $\bar{p}_2$ (see figure A2.2, which describes the demand (D) for commodity 2 at different prices). This means that the consumer is now confronted by a budget line AC in figure A2.1 and thus has a possibility of reaching a higher indifference curve than at point A. To move from A to the new optimum position at point B, he pays for $\bar{x}_2$ an amount corresponding to $x_1^* - \bar{x}_1$ of commodity 1 ('other goods') or corresponding to $\bar{p}_2 \bar{x}_2$ in figure A2.2. But it can be shown that the consumer is willing to pay more than this amount for the possibility of buying commodity 2 at price $\bar{p}_2$. In other words, he has a *consumer's surplus*, which is the maximum he would give up rather than go without the availability of commodity 2 at price $\bar{p}_2$. More specifically, figure A2.1 shows that the consumer is willing to pay (in addition to the price $\bar{p}_2$) a lump sum or an 'entrance fee' up to $x_1^* - \tilde{x}_1$; the explanation is that he may allow his disposable income to drop by this amount, that is, allow his budget line to shift downwards accordingly, without ending up in a worse position (on a lower indifference curve) than at the initial point A. But if he now actually had to part with (almost) all of his consumer's surplus, he would no longer be willing to buy quantity $\bar{x}_2$ of commodity 2, but only $\bar{\bar{x}}_2$. Thus, in this particular case he would

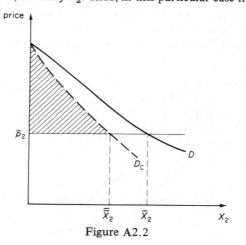

Figure A2.2

only demand $\bar{\bar{x}}_2$ at the price $\bar{p}_2$. In reality, he would then pay an 'entrance fee' = consumer's surplus = $x_1^* - \tilde{x}_1$ as well as the amount $\bar{p}_2\bar{\bar{x}}_2$, or, *in toto*, $x_1^* - \bar{\tilde{x}}_1$.

Now that we have explained the exact meaning of the consumer's surplus in terms of figure A2.1, let us try to relate the surplus concept to the individual demand curve in figure A2.2. Firstly, it should be noted that the above argument would apply equally well for prices other than $\bar{p}_2$. In fact, for any price p_2 we would have been able to establish a quantity corresponding to $\bar{\bar{x}}_2$, that is a quantity of commodity 2 demanded by the individual if he had had to part with his consumer's surplus in the form of an 'entrance fee' (the size of the surplus would, of course, vary with the price charged). In this way we would have been able to generate a complete curve of such price–quantity combinations, a so-called compensated demand curve, as illustrated by the D_c curve in figure A2.2. We are satisfied here with the statement that it can be proved that the consumer's surplus in each case equals the area under this particular 'demand curve' D_c down to the relevant price level. The shaded area in figure A2.2 thus shows the size of the consumer's surplus at $p_2 = \bar{p}_2$, that is the equivalent of $x_1^* - \bar{x}_1$ in figure A2.1.

We now know which area under what curve defines the exact size of the consumer's surplus. The next step is to note that the D_c curve is often close enough to the D curve for the area under the latter curve—the ordinary demand curve—to give a reasonably good approximation of the consumer's surplus. If the budget lines in figure A2.1 had touched the indifference curves (I^1 and I^2, respectively) at the same quantity of x_2, say $\bar{x}_2$, so that the individual consumer would demand $\bar{x}_2$ of commodity 2 regardless of his level of income, the two curves D and D_c would in fact have coincided. Thus, in this special case (where the income elasticity of commodity 2 can be seen to be zero) the area under the ordinary demand curve and the size of the consumer's surplus would be identical.

So far we have only dealt with the individual consumer's surplus. The investment criteria for which we need the concept of consumer's surplus permit a straightforward addition of all individual consumer's surpluses only if the prevailing income distribution is acceptable to the policy makers. (The same restriction applies, of course, to the summation of ordinary market payments; they cannot be added to obtain a relevant estimate of the revenue or benefit side of an investment project if the distribution of income were considered unacceptable by the government). If the prevailing income distribution is not acceptable, an aggregate consumers' surplus could be obtained, at least in principle, by first multiplying each individual consumer's surplus by a factor expressing how the policy maker values an increase in the welfare of each individual or group (see also footnote 1, page 111).

REFERENCES

A. Required Reading

As pointed out in the Preface, some elementary knowledge of the economic theory of consumer behaviour and firm behaviour is required in order to assimilate the text as a whole. The required elements can be found, for example, in

Samuelson, P.A. (1970). *Economics*, 8th ed., McGraw-Hill, New York, chapters 19, 21, 22 and 25.

or
> Lipsey, R. and Steiner, P. (1972). *Economics,* Harper & Row, London, chapters 8, 11 and 13, in particular.

B. Further Reading

There are relatively few comprehensive, introductive presentations of 'welfare economics'. The following texts, covering most of the subject matter, can be recommended.
> Baumol, W. (1972). *Economic Theory and Operations Analysis,* Irwin, Englewood Cliffs;
> Scitovsky, T. (1971). *Welfare and Competition,* Allen & Unwin, London;

or, on a more advanced level,
> Graaff, J. (1967). *Theoretical Welfare Economics,* Cambridge University Press, London;
> Arrow, K. and Scitovsky, T. (1969). *Readings in Welfare Economics,* Allen & Unwin, London.

For applications to socialist economies see
> Lerner, A. (1947). *Economics of Control,* New York;
> Lange, O. (1952). *On the Economic Theory of Socialism* in Lange, O. and Taylor, F. (eds.) *The Economic Theory of Socialism,* Minneapolis.

Recommended readings concerning the subject matter in each chapter of this book:

Chapter 1

The conditions for Pareto optimality are derived and discussed in
> Bator, F.M. (1957). The Simple analytics of welfare maximization. *American Economic Review,* March 1957 or in Breit, W. and Hochman, H. (1969). *Readings in Microeconomics,* Holt, London;
> Winch, D.M. (1971). *Analytical Welfare Economics,* Penguin, Harmondsworth);

and on a more advanced level:
> Henderson, J.M. and Quandt, R.E. (1971). *Microeconomic Theory,* McGraw-Hill, New York, chapter 7;
> Samuelson, P.A. (1948). *Foundations of Economic Analysis,* Harvard University Press, Cambridge, Mass., chapter 8.

The conditions under which there is a correspondence between Pareto optimum and general equilibrium in a market economy are discussed rigorously and with advanced mathematics in
> Debreu, G. (1962). *Theory of Value,* Wiley, New York.

Chapter 2

A general and fairly simple survey of market imperfections and their implications is given in

Bator, F.M. (1958). The anatomy of market failure. *Quarterly Journal of Economics*, Aug. 1958 or in Breit, W. and Hochman, H., *op. cit.*

External effects (2.1) are discussed in detail in
Buchanan, J.M. and Stubblebine, W.C. (1962). Externality. *Economica*, November 1962 or in Breit, W. and Hochman, H., *op. cit.*;
Bohm, P. (1967). *External Economics in Production*, Almqvist & Wiksell, Stockholm;
Mishan, E.J. (1971). The postwar literature on externalities. *Journal of Economic Literature*, March 1971.

For an application of externality theory in the field of environmental economics see, for example,
Kneese, A.V. and Bower, B.T. (1968). *Managing Water Quality*, Johns Hopkins, Baltimore.

Allocation problems in connection with *public goods* (section 2.2) are discussed in
Buchanan, J.M. (1969). *The Demand and Supply of Public Goods*, Chicago;
Peston, M. (1972). *Public Goods and the Public Sector*, Macmillan, London.

A more advanced and condensed treatment is found in
McGuire, M. and Aaron, H. (1969). Efficiency and equity in the optimal supply of a public good. *Review of Economics and Statistics*, Feb. 1969.

The problem of estimating demand for public goods is discussed in the context of an experiment in
Bohm, P. (1972). Estimating demand for public goods: an experiment. *European Economic Review*, No. 3, 1972.

The efficiency problems arising from *economies of scale* or decreasing average costs (section 2.3) are analysed in
Oort, C.J. (1958). *Decreasing Costs as a Problem of Welfare Economics*, North Holland, Amsterdam;

and in the context of an application to the transportation field
Walters, A.A. (1968). *The Economics of Road User Charges*, IBRD, Baltimore.

Allocative inefficiency due to market *disequilibrium* (section 2.5) is analysed in two applications in
Lindbeck, A. (1967). *Rent Control as an Instrument of Housing Policy* in Nevitt, A. (ed.) *Economic Problems of Housing*, London;
Bohm, P. (1968). *Pricing of Copper in International Trade — A Problem of Price Stabilization*, Norstedts, Stockholm.

Efficiency aspects of *imperfect competition* (section 2.6) are found in
    Rowley, C. (1973). *Antitrust and Economic Efficiency,* Macmillan, Lond
Economic aspects of *information* (section 2.7) are discussed in
    Lamberton, D.M. (1971). *Economics of Information and Knowledge,*
    Penguin, Harmondsworth;
    Marschak, J. and Radner, R. (1972). *Economic Theory of Teams,*
    Yale University Press, New Haven.

Problems of *'second-best'*, that is, allocation problems in the presence
of constraints on allocation policy (section 2.8) are analysed, for example, in
    Lipsey, R. and Lancaster, K. (1956-7). The general theory of second
    best. *Review of Economic Studies,* 24 (1956-7);
    Davis, O.A. and Whinston, A. (1965). Welfare economics and the
    theory of second best. *Review of Economic Studies,* 32 (Jan.
    1965);
    Bohm, P. (1967). On the theory of second best. *Review of Economic
    Studies,* 34 (1967).

Chapter 3

An introduction to the *effects of various forms of taxes on allocation*
(section 3.1) is given by
    Johansen, L. (1965). *Public Economics,* North Holland, Amsterdam,
    chapter VII.6 and
    Musgrave, R. (1959). *Theory of Public Finance,* McGraw-Hill, New
    York, chapter 12.

Efficiency aspects of distribution policy (section 3.2) are analysed, for
example, in
    (section 3.2.1) Green, C. (1967). *Negative Taxes and the Poverty Problem*
    Brookings, Washington;
    (section 3.2.3) Bohm, P. (1968). Time horizons and terminal capital,
    Swedish Journal of Economics, Dec. 1968.

Chapter 4

For an informative presentation of *applied* cost–benefit analysis see,
for example,
    Krutilla, J. and Eckstein, O. (1958). *Multiple Purpose River Develop-
    ment,* Johns Hopkins, Baltimore, Part II;
    Foster, C.D. and Beesley, M.E. (1963). Estimating the social benefit
    of constructing an underground railway in London. *Journal of
    the Royal Statistical Society,* Part 1, 1963.

For more detailed presentations of the *theory* of cost–benefit analysis
see, for example,
    Maass, A. (1962). *Design of Water Resource Development,* Harvard
    Univ. Press, London, chapters 2 and 4 (especially pp. 17-58);
    Mishan, E. J. (1972). *Elements of Cost–Benefit Analysis,* Allen &
    Unwin, London.

INDEX